MW01240526

THE SUBCONSCIOUS AND THE SUPERCONSCIOUS PLANES OF MIND

WILLIAM WALKER ATKINSON

2015 by McAllister Editions (MCALLISTEREDITIONS@GMAIL.COM). This book is a classic, and a product of its time. It does not reflect the same views on race, gender, sexuality, ethnicity, and interpersonal relations as it would if it was written today.

CONTENTS

1

Infra-Conscious Mentality.

The great problems of modern psychology are found to consist largely of the phenomena of the mental operations and activities on planes other than those of ordinary consciousness. While the terminology of the subject is still in a state of transition, nevertheless certain terms have sprung into common use and are employed tentatively by those who write and teach of these wonderful regions of the mind. Among these terms we find "infra-conscious," which is used to designate the planes of mental activity below and above the ordinary plane of consciousness. In this term, the word "infra" is used in the sense of inner, within, etc., rather than its more familiar sense of "below." Hence "infra-conscious" means an inner consciousness, or within-consciousness, and includes the mental planes commonly known as the "*sub* conscious" and "*super* conscious," respectively. The term is far from being satisfactory, but it is used by psychologists, tentatively, and will be until some other more fitting term is evolved.

The older school of psychology ignored, so far as possible, the infra-conscious planes and fields of mental activity, and regarded consciousness as synonymous with mind—and by "consciousness" was meant merely the plane of the ordinary consciousness. But the phenomena of the hidden planes of mentation would not stay in the dark corner in which the psychologists were compelled to place them, but would constantly present themselves most inopportunely, as if to perplex the teachers, and to confute their theories. And so, little by little, there was tacitly admitted to exist an unknown and unexplored region of the mind which was at first labeled "unconscious mind," although the term was vigorously opposed by many of the authorities as contradictory and meaningless— but the quarrel was rather with the term than with the fact.

The psychologists who began to use the term "unconscious mind" soon found sufficient authority among certain of the older writers, which served as a foundation for the newer theories and teachings which began to evolve when the conception of the "unconscious mind" had begun to take upon itself the garb of scientific orthodoxy. It was found that Leibnitz had asserted that there were certain mental activities in evidence, which certainly manifested in the "unconscious" region of the mind, and the influence of the older philosopher was added to the new teaching. As Carpenter said: "The psychologists of Germany, from the time of Leibnitz, have taught that much of our mental work is done without consciousness." Sir William Hamilton said: "To this great philosopher (Leibnitz) belongs the honor of having originated this opinion, and of having supplied some of the strongest arguments in its support." Kay said: "Leibnitz was the first to confute this opinion (that consciousness was coextensive with mind), and to establish the doctrine that there are energies always at work, and modifications constantly taking place in the mind, of which we are quite unconscious."

Basing the new conception upon Leibnitz and his followers, the psychologist began to write freely regarding this great "unconscious" area of the mind. But, nevertheless, it was regarded by many of the more conservative authorities as an unwarrantable extension of psychological inquiry into a field which properly belonged to metaphysics. Schofield says: "So many psychologists—the high priests of the religion of mind— being committed so generally to deny and refuse any extension of it outside consciousness, though they cannot refrain from what Ribot calls 'a sly glance' at the forbidden fruit, consistently ignore the existence of the Unconscious, their pupils naturally treading in their steps; while the physician of the period, reveling in the multiplication and elaboration of physical methods of diagnosis and experiment, is led to despise and contemptuously set aside as 'only fancy' those psychical agencies which can cure, if they cannot diagnose. It may be asked, why was not an attempt made sooner to give these unconscious faculties their proper place? It *was* made determinedly years ago in Germany, and since then in England, by men who, to their honor undeterred by ridicule and contempt, made noble and partially successful efforts to establish the truth."

But we may find many important references to this great "unconscious" area of mind in the writings of the earlier of the older writers on the subject in the Nineteenth Century. Sir William Hamilton,

2

Lewes, Carpenter and others referred freely to it, and taught it as a truth of psychology. Lewes said: "The teaching of most modern psychologists is that consciousness forms but a small item in the total of psychical processes. Unconscious sensations, ideas and judgments are made to play a great part in their explanations. It is very certain that in every conscious volition—every act that is so characterized—the larger part of it is quite unconscious. It is equally certain that in every perception there are unconscious processes of reproduction and inference,—there is a middle distance of subconsciousness, and a background of unconsciousness." Sir William Hamilton said: "I do not hesitate to affirm that what we are conscious of is constructed out of what we are not conscious of—that our whole knowledge in fact is made up of the unknown and incognizable. The sphere of our consciousness is only a small circle in the centre of a far wider sphere of action and passion, of which we are only conscious through its effects.... The fact of such latent mental modifications is now established beyond a rational doubt; and, on the supposition of their reality, we are able to solve various psychological phenomena otherwise inexplicable."

Taine said: "Mental events imperceptible to consciousness are far more numerous than the others, and of the world which makes up our being we only perceive the highest points—the lighted-up peaks of a continent whose lower levels remain in the shade. Beneath ordinary sensations are their components— that is to say, the elementary sensations, which must be combined into groups to reach our consciousness. Outside a little luminous circle lies a large ring of twilight, and beyond this an indefinite night; but the events of this twilight and this night are as real as those within the luminous circle." Maudsley says: "Examine closely, and without bias, the ordinary mental operations of daily life, and you will surely discover that consciousness has not one-tenth part of the function therein which it is commonly assumed to have...In every conscious state there are at work conscious, sub-conscious, and infra-conscious energies, the last as indispensable as the first."

Kay said: "Every impression or thought that has once been before consciousness remains ever after impressed in the mind. It may never again come up before consciousness, but it will doubtless remain in that vast ultra-conscious region of the mind, unconsciously moulding and fashioning our subsequent thoughts and actions. It is only a small part of what exists in the mind that we are at any time conscious of. There is always much that is known to be in the mind that exists in it unconsciously, and must be stored away somewhere. We may be able to recall it into consciousness when we wish to do so, but at other times the mind is unconscious of its existence."

Morrell said: "We have every reason to believe that mental power when once called forth follows the analogy of everything we see in the material universe in the fact of its perpetuity. Every single effort of mind is a creation which can never go back again into nonentity. It may slumber in the depths of forgetfulness as light and heat slumber in the coal seams, but there it is, ready at the bidding of some appropriate stimulus to come again out of the darkness into the light of consciousness.... What is termed 'common sense' is nothing but a substratum of experiences out of which our judgments flow, while the experiences themselves are hidden away in the unconscious depths of our intellectual nature; and even the flow of public opinion is formed by ideas which lie tacitly in the national mind, and come into consciousness, generally, a long time after they have been really operating and shaping the course of events in human history." Carpenter said: "Man's ordinary common-sense is the resultant of the unconscious co-ordination of a long succession of small experiences mostly forgotten, or perhaps never brought out into distinct consciousness."

The study of the subject of Memory led many of the psychologists of the last generation to assume as a necessity the existence of a great "unconscious" storehouse in which all the records impressed upon the mind were preserved. Other branches of psychology forced their investigators to assume a great area of the mind, lying outside of the field of consciousness, to account for certain phenomena. And, so, gradually the idea of the existence of this undiscovered and unexplored country of the mind came to be accepted as orthodox by all except the ultra-conservatives, and investigation in the said direction was encouraged instead of discouraged or forbidden as has been the case previously. And arising from the thought on the subject of the "un-conscious mind" we find the evolving conception of there being various strata, planes, or regions of mind of varying stages of consciousness—that, instead of there being but *one* plane of consciousness, there were *many*—that instead of there being an "unconscious region" there was one, or more, additional plane of consciousness, operating under general laws and being as much a part of the general consciousness as is that plane which we speak of as the ordinary consciousness.

This was the beginning of the various dual-mind theories, which we shall now consider.

2
The Manifold Mind.

Arising naturally from the speculations regarding the "unconscious mind" we find the conception of the "dual-mind" taking a prominent place on the stage of psychological consideration. From the idea of an unconscious area of mind was evolved the conception of *two minds* possessed by the individual, each independent and yet both working together in the production of mental phenomena. It is difficult to determine the beginning of this conception. Traces of it and vague hints regarding it may be found in many of the earlier writings. While there seems to have been a dawning conception of the subconscious mind as a separate mind on the part of many thinkers and writers in the latter part of the Twentieth Century, yet to two men must be given the credit of attracting the public notice to the subject, and of the presentation of the thought in a positive, clear form. We refer to Frederic W. H. Myers and Thomson J. Hudson, respectively. Both of these men offered a dual-mind theory or working hypothesis as a basis for a correct understanding of what has been called "Psychic Phenomena," by which is meant the phenomena of telepathy, clairvoyance, hypnotism, trance-conditions, etc.

Myers evolved the idea that the self was not only a unity but was also a coordination, and that it "possesses faculties and powers unexercised and unexercisable by the consciousness that finds employment in the direction of the affairs of every-day life," as Bruce so well states it. In 1887 he first made public his theory of the "Subliminal Self," as he called this secondary or hidden mind. After that time, for several years, he wrote and spoke frequently on the subject, and in the year last mentioned his full theory was embodied in his work entitled "Human Personality," which was published after his death.

Myers stated his conception of the Subliminal Self in his great work, as follows: "The idea of a *threshold* (limen, Schwelle) of consciousness—of a level above which sensation or thought must rise before it can enter into our conscious life—is a simple and familiar one. The word *subliminal*—meaning 'beneath the threshold'—has already been used to

6

define those sensations which are too feeble to be individually recognized. I propose to extend the meaning of the term, so as to make it cover *all* that takes place beneath the ordinary threshold, or say, if preferred, the ordinary margin of consciousness—not only those faint stimulations whose very faintness keeps them submerged, but much else which psychology as yet scarcely recognizes—sensations, thoughts, emotions, which may be strong, definite and independent; but which, by the original constitution of our being, seldom merge into that *supraliminal* current of consciousness which we habitually identify with *ourselves.* Perceiving that these submerged thoughts and emotions possess the characteristics which we associate with conscious life, I feel bound to speak of a *subliminal,* or *ultramarginal,* consciousness—a consciousness which we shall see, for instance, uttering or writing sentences quite as complex and coherent as the supraliminal consciousness could make them. Perceiving further that this conscious life beneath the threshold or beneath the margin seems to be no discontinuous or intermittent thing; that not only are these isolated subliminal processes comparable with isolated supraliminal processes (as when a problem is solved by some unknown procedure in a dream), but that there also is a continuous subliminal chain of memory (or more chains than one) involving just that kind of individual and persistent revival of old impressions and response to new ones, which we commonly call a Self—I find it permissible and convenient to speak of subliminal Selves or more briefly of a Subliminal Self. I do not intend by using this term assume that there are two correlative and parallel selves existing always within each of us. Rather I mean by the Subliminal Self that part of the Self which is commonly subliminal; and I conceive that there may be—not only *cooperations* between these quasi-independent trains of thought—but also upheavals and alternations of personality of many kinds, so that what was once below the surface may for a time, or permanently, rise above it. And I conceive also that no Self of which we can here have cognizance, is in reality more than a fragment of a larger Self—revealed in a fashion at once shifting and limited through an organism not so framed as to afford it full manifestation."

Perhaps to Hudson, even more than to Myers, is due the wide-spread interest in the dual-mind theory or conception. In 1893, Hudson, in his work entitled "The Law of Psychic Phenomena," boldly enunciated his now famous theory of the "Subjective Mind," which at once caught the popular fancy, and which he elaborated in his subsequent works. Hudson's dual-mind theory can best be stated in his own words. In his work, above mentioned, he states: "Man has, or appears to have, two minds, each endowed with separate and distinct attributes and powers; each capable, under certain conditions, of independent action. It should be clearly understood at the outset "that for the purpose of arriving at a conclusion it is a matter of indifference whether we consider that man is endowed with two distinct minds, or that his one mind possesses certain attributes and powers under some conditions, and certain other attributes and powers under other conditions. It is sufficient to know that everything happens just as though he were endowed with a dual mental organization. Under the rules of correct reasoning, therefore, I have a right to assume that *man has two minds*; and the assumption is so stated, in its broadest terms, as the first proposition of my hypothesis. For convenience, I shall designate the one as the *objective* mind, and the other as the *subjective* mind." We shall consider the details of Hudson's theory in another chapter.

Following Hudson and Myers came a number of other writers who eagerly availed themselves of the convenient classification of the mind into two divisions or "two minds."

The new hypothesis served as an excellent foundation for various theories explaining, or attempting to explain, all things "in heaven and in earth" ever dreamt of in any of the philosophies. Some of the wildest theories were built upon this broad foundation, and this fact caused many careful thinkers to undervalue the fundamental principles of both Myers' and Hudson's thought. Hudson, himself, alienated a number of his earlier admirers by extending his theory to what was considered unwarranted lengths in his later books in which he boldly invaded the metaphysical and theological fields, endeavoring to account for and explain immortality and the "divine pedigree" by his dual-mind theory. And Myers, by identifying his theory with the phenomena of Telepathy, brought down on his head the adverse criticism of the orthodox psychologists, so that the value of his conception was largely overlooked.

But there were other influences at work which led to the gradual recognition of the fact that while Myers' and Hudson's conceptions served an excellent purpose of classification and convenience of thought, nevertheless they must properly be regarded as but the first steps toward a larger and more complete theory. It was recognized that the subconscious mind (under its various names) could scarcely be at one and the same time the seat of emotional impulses, suggested vagaries, delusions, etc., and also the region of the highest intuition, spiritual truth, and other mental and spiritual qualities which seemed to be *above* rather than *below* the ordinary mind of man. To this dissatisfaction the teaching of Vivekananda, and other Hindu teachers visiting America and Europe, contributed.

These Oriental teachers taught that just as there was a *sub*consciousness, below the ordinary plane of consciousness, so was there a *super*consciousness, above the ordinary plane. From the one emerged the things which had been deposited there by race-inheritance, suggestion, memory, etc., while from the other came things which had never been placed there by either race-experience or individual experience but which were superimposed from higher regions of the soul. These newer ideas gave to the "three-mind" conception advantages lacking in the "two-mind" theory.

Then came a reconciliation in the writings of various investigators and teachers who held that the mind of man consisted of *many* regions, some *higher* and some *lower* than the ordinary plane of consciousness. In short, the most advanced thought of to-day on the subject holds that the mind of man consists of many planes of mentation, in which are manifested the phenomena of subconsciousness and superconsciousness, in great variety and degree. And the minds of thousands of earnest investigators are now bent upon an exploration of these vast, unknown regions of the mind.

Sir Oliver Lodge has aptly and beautifully expressed the most advanced conception of the various planes of the human mind in his well-known paragraph: "Imagine an iceberg glorying in its crisp solidity and sparkling pinnacles, resenting attention paid to its submerged self, or supporting region, or to the saline liquid out of which it arose, and into which in due course it will someday return. Or, reversing the metaphor, we may liken our present state to that of the bull of a ship submerged in a dim ocean among strange monsters, propelled in a blind manner through space; proud perhaps of accumulating many barnacles of decoration; only recognizing our destination by bumping against the dock-wall; and with no cognizance of the deck and cabins above us, or to the spars and sails—no thought of the sextant and the compass, and the captain—no perception of the lookout on the mast—of the distant horizon. With no visions of objects far ahead—dangers to be avoided—destinations to be reached—other ships to be spoken to by means other than bodily contact—a region of sunshine and cloud, of space, or perception, and of intelligence utterly inaccessible below the water line."

Dr. Schofield also paints us a beautiful word-picture of the same conditions, in words which should be always considered in connection with the paragraph of Sir Oliver Lodge, just quoted. Here are Schofield's words: "Our conscious mind, as compared with the unconscious mind, has been likened to the visible spectrum of the sun's rays, as compared to the invisible part which stretches indefinitely on either side. We know now that the chief part of heat comes from the ultra-red rays that show no light; and the main part of the chemical changes in the vegetable world are the results of the ultra-violet rays at the other end of the spectrum, which are equally invisible to the eye, and are recognized only by their potent effects. Indeed as these visible rays extend indefinitely on both sides of the visible spectrum, so we may say that the mind includes not only the visible or conscious part, and what we have termed the subconscious, that which lies below the red line, but also the supra-conscious mind that lies at the other end—all those regions of higher soul and spirit life, of which we are only at times vaguely conscious, but which always exist, and link us on to eternal verities, on the one side, as surely as the subconscious mind links us to the body on the other."

Keeping before us then the fact that there are regions *above*, as well as *below* (and also, probably, regions *parallel* to) our ordinary consciousness, let us now proceed to a consideration of what has been gathered by the many investigators regarding these strange regions of the Self. Let us examine the various reports before formulating a *theory*—let us examine the various theses and antitheses before we attempt to synthesize.

3
Hudson's "Subjective Mind."

Hudson, in his conception of the "subjective mind," not only postulated the existence of a plane of mentality, or a "mind," in which was performed the subconscious activities recognized by the later psychologists, but also held that in that mind were manifested the unusual and almost abnormal activities which are generally grouped together under the term "Psychic Phenomena." In fact this explanation of psychic phenomena by the theory or hypothesis of the subjective mind was the main purpose and underlying idea in his principal work, as is indicated by its title: "The Law of Psychic Phenomena." In order to understand the general subject of the subconscious mind, and its phenomena, it is necessary that the general idea of Hudson be considered, for its influence has been very marked on the later writings on the subject.

Hudson advanced as a working hypothesis the general proposition of the *dual-mind*. The statement of the duality of mind, and the naming of its phases as the *objective* and *subjective* minds, respectively, is the first proposition of his hypothesis. He then proceeds as follows: "The second proposition is, that the subjective mind *is constantly amenable to control by suggestion.*

The third, or subsidiary, proposition is, that the subjective mind *is incapable of inductive reasoning.*" He then explains his use of the terms objective mind and subjective mind, which usage was opposed to that familiar to the older psychologists and which aroused instant opposition from them. Hudson states:

"In general terms the difference between man's two minds may be stated as follows:—The objective mind takes cognizance of the objective world. Its media of observation are the five physical senses. It is the outgrowth of man's physical necessities. It is his guide in his struggle with his material environment. Its highest function is that of reasoning. The subjective mind takes cognizance of its environment by means independent of the physical senses. It perceives by intuition. It is the seat of the emotions, and the storehouse of memory. It performs its highest functions when the objective senses are in abeyance. In a word, it is that intelligence which makes itself manifest in a hypnotic subject when he is in a state of somnambulism. In this state many of the most wonderful feats of the subjective mind are performed. It sees without the natural organs of vision; and in this, as in many other grades, or degrees, of the hypnotic state, it can be made, apparently, to leave the body, and travel to distant lands and bring back intelligence, ofttimes of the most exact and truthful character. It also has the power to read the thoughts of others, even to the minutest details; to read the contents of sealed envelopes and closed books. In short it is the subjective mind that possesses what is popularly designated as clairvoyant power, and the ability to apprehend the thoughts of others without the aid of the ordinary means of communication. In point of fact, that which for convenience I have chosen to designate, as the subjective mind appears to be a separate and distinct entity; and the real distinctive difference between the two minds seems to consist in the fact that the objective mind is merely the function of the physical brain, while the subjective mind is a distinct entity, possessing independent powers and functions, having a mental organization of its own, and being capable of sustaining an existence independently of the body. In other words, *it is the soul*."

After making the above startling statement that the subjective mind is not only a separate entity, but is in fact *the soul*, Dr. Hudson then proceeds with his second proposition, that the subjective mind is constantly amenable to control by suggestion. He states the matter as follows:

"1. That the objective mind, or, let us say, man in his normal condition is not controllable, against reason, positive knowledge, or the evidence of his senses, by the suggestions of another.

2. That the subjective mind, or man in the hypnotic state, is unqualifiedly and constantly amenable to the power of suggestion. That is to say, the subjective mind accepts, without hesitation or doubt, every statement that is made to it, no matter how absurd or incongruous or contrary to the objective experience of the individual.... These are fundamental facts, known and acknowledged by every student of the science of hypnotism."

We may say here in passing, that this last statement of the "fundamental facts, known and acknowledged by every student of hypnotism" is now vigorously opposed by many leading authorities on suggestion. While it is true that in certain stages of hypnosis the deeper strata of the subconscious region of mind are tapped, it is likewise true that suggestion does not depend upon the hypnotic condition, but on the contrary is manifested in the waking state. And, likewise Dr. Hudson's statement that "The objective mind...is not controllable...by the suggestions of another" is not now accepted as correct by leading authorities upon suggestion; for it is known that the objective mind *is* amenable to suggestion, and that much of the phenomena of suggestion is manifested in this plane of the mind. It is true, however, that much of the difference of opinion seemingly arises from the confusion of terms, and the definition of "suggestion." Moreover, Dr. Hudson's theory is not seriously affected by the above objection, and the value of his classification is not impaired.

Dr. Hudson then proceeds to explain another characteristic of the subjective mind—his third proposition. He says: "One of the most important distinctions between the objective and subjective minds pertains to the function of reason.... (1)

The Objective Mind is capable of reasoning by all methods—inductive and deductive, analytic and synthetic. (2) The subjective mind is incapable of inductive reasoning. Let it here be understood that this proposition refers to the powers and functions of the purely subjective mind, as exhibited in the mental operations in persons in a state of profound hypnotism or trance.

The prodigious intellectual feats of persons in that condition have been a source of amazement in all the ages; but the striking peculiarity noted above appears to have been lost sight of in admiration of the other qualities exhibited. In other words, it has never been noted that their reasoning is always deductive, or syllogistic. The subjective mind never classifies a series of known facts, and reasons from them up to general principles; but, given a general principle to start with, it will reason deductively from that down to all legitimate inferences, with a marvelous cogency and power. Place a man of intelligence and cultivation in a hypnotic state, and give him a premise—say in the form of a statement of a general principle of philosophy; and no matter what may have been his opinions in his normal condition, he will unhesitatingly, in obedience to the power of suggestion, assume the correctness of the proposition; and if given an opportunity to discuss the question, will proceed to deduce therefrom the details of a whole system of philosophy. Every conclusion will be so clearly and logically deducible from the major premise, and withal so plausible and consistent, that the listener will almost forget that the premise was assumed."

Dr. Hudson also claimed for the subjective mind that it possessed "a prodigious memory." He states: "It would perhaps be hazardous to say that the memory of the subjective mind is perfect, but there is good ground for believing that such a proposition would be substantially true." He also states further on in his book that: "The irresistible inference is that when the soul is freed entirely from its trammels of flesh, its powers will attain perfection, its memory will be absolute.... Subjective memory appears to be the only kind or quality of memory which deserves that appellation; it is the only memory which is absolute. The memory of the objective mind, comparatively speaking, is more properly designated as recollection."

In his later books Dr. Hudson sought to establish the Immortality of the Soul by his theory of the subjective mind, which latter he identified with the soul. He also sought to prove the Divine Pedigree of Man by the same theory, holding practically that God's attributes and characteristics must be practically those of the subjective mind raised to infinity. With these questions we have no concern in this work. Many of Dr. Hudson's most ardent admirers express the opinion that he had carried his idea too far—having assumed a premise, he carried it to its extreme conclusion, in the very manner which he himself claimed for the subjective mind itself, as stated in a quotation on a preceding page. We shall not discuss this question, as it forms no part of the subject of our present consideration.

Many of the best authorities to-day, while giving to Dr. Hudson the highest praise for his valuable work of classification and presentation of collected data, feel that he was without warrant for assuming the subjective mind to be a separate entity, in fact *the soul*. They are of the opinion that he has made the mistake of collating the phenomena of several widely-separated planes or phases of the mind, high and low, and then grouping them together as qualities of a separate entity distinct from the objective mind. The trend of the latest and most advanced thought on the subject is that not only the various subconscious planes, and superconscious planes of the mind, but also the so-called objective mind itself, are but phases or planes of manifestation of *one mind*, or self, of the individual. It is held that if we separate the various planes of mental manifestation into separate entities, we shall have not *two minds* but *many minds*. The mind is held to be far more complex than is indicated by any *two-mind* theory. But, as we have said, the work of Dr. Hudson is highly esteemed although his conclusions are not now generally adopted or accepted. He has done more than any other recent writer on the subject to popularize the idea of subconscious mentality and to render familiar the phenomena thereof.

4
Unconscious Cerebration.

Perhaps the nature of the Infra-conscious planes of mentation may be better understood by reference to the observed phenomena of those planes than by the consideration of any special theories regarding them. Therefore we shall devote considerable space in this book to a presentation of instances of the activities of these planes.

Carpenter calls attention to the common experience of subconscious mentation and illustrates it by the experience of a friend who stated that at one time he had laboriously sought for the solution of a difficult problem, but without success. Then suddenly the solution flashed across his mind, and so complete was the answer and so unexpected was its appearance that he trembled as if in the presence of another being who had communicated a secret to him. Rosmini says of this action of the mind: "A close attention to our internal operations, along with induction, gives us this result, that we even exercise ratiocination of which we have no consciousness, and generally it furnishes us with this marvelous law, that every operation whatsoever of our minds is unknown to itself until a second operation reveals it to us." Noah Porter says: "That the soul may act without being conscious of what it does and that these unconscious acts affect those acts of which it is conscious has been already established."

Wundt says: "The unconscious logical processes are carried on with a certainty and regularity which would be impossible where there exists the possibility of error. Our mind is so happily designed that it prepares for us the most important foundations of cognition, whilst we have not the slightest apprehension of the *modus operandi*. This unconscious soul, like a benevolent stranger, works and makes provision for our benefit, pouring only the mature fruits into our laps. Bascom says: "It is inexplicable how premises which lie below consciousness can sustain conclusions in consciousness; how the mind can wittingly take up a mental movement at an advanced stage, having missed its primary steps." Maudsley says: "It is surprising how uncomfortable a person may be made by the obscure idea of something which he ought to have said or

16

done, and which he cannot for the life of him remember. There is the effort of the lost idea to get into consciousness, which is relieved directly the idea bursts into consciousness."

Oliver Wendell Holmes says: "There are thoughts that never emerge into consciousness, which yet make their influence felt among the perceptive mental currents just as the unseen planets sway the movements of the known ones...I was told of a business man in Boston who had given up thinking of an important question as too much for him. But he continued so uneasy in his brain he feared he was threatened with palsy. After some hours the natural solution of the question came to him, worked out, as he believed, in that troubled interval."

Schofield says: "Last year the writer was driving to Phillimore Gardens to give some letters to a friend. On the way a vague uneasiness sprang up, and a voice seemed to say, 'I doubt if you have those letters.' Conscious reason rebuked it and said, 'Of course you have; you took them out of the drawer specially.' The vague feeling was not satisfied, but could not reply. On arrival, he found the letters were in none of his pockets. On returning, they were found on the hall table, where they had been placed a moment while putting on his gloves. The other day the writer had to go to see a patient in Folkstone, in Shakespeare Terrace. He got there very late, and did not stay but drove down to the Pavilion for the night, it being dark and rainy. Next morning at eleven he walked up to find the house, knowing the general direction, though never having walked there before. He went up the main road, and after passing a certain turning, began to feel a vague uneasiness coming into consciousness, that he had passed the terrace. On asking the way, he found it was so; and the turning was where the uneasiness began. The night before was pitch dark and very wet, and anything seen from a close carriage was quite unconsciously impressed on his mind."

Kirchener says: "Our consciousness can only grasp one, quite clear idea at once. All other ideas are for the time somewhat obscure. They are really existing, but only potentially for consciousness; i. e., they hover as it were, on our horizon, or beneath the threshold of consciousness. The fact that former ideas suddenly return to consciousness is simply explained by the fact that they have continued psychic existence; and attention is sometimes voluntarily or involuntarily turned away from the present, and the reappearance of former ideas is thus made possible." Holmes says: "Our different ideas are stepping-stones; how we get from one to another we do not know; something carries us. We (our conscious selves) do not take the step. The creating and informing spirit, which is *within* us and not *of* us, is recognized everywhere in real life. It comes to us as a voice that will be heard; it tells us what we must believe; it frames our sentences and we wonder at this visitor who chooses our brain as his dwelling-place."

Montgomery says: "We are constantly aware that feelings emerge unsolicited by any previous mental state, directly from the dark womb of unconsciousness. Indeed all our most vivid feelings are thus mystically derived. Suddenly a new irrelevant, unwilled, unlooked-for presence intrudes itself into consciousness. Some inscrutable power causes it to rise and enter the mental presence as a sensorial constituent. If this vivid dependence on unconscious forces has to be conjectured with regard to the most vivid mental occurrences, how much more must such a sustaining foundation be postulated for those faint revivals of previous sensations that so largely assist in making up our complex mental presence!" Brodie says: "It has often happened to me to have accumulated a store of facts, but to have been able to proceed no further. Then, after an interval of time, I have found the obscurity and confusion to have cleared away; the facts to have settled in their right places, though I have not been sensible of having made any effort for that purpose."

Von Hartmann says: "What Schopenhauer calls 'unconscious rumination' regularly happens to me when I have read a work which presents new points of view essentially opposed to my previous opinions…. After days, weeks, or months we find, to our great astonishment, that the old opinions we had held up to that moment have been entirely rearranged, and that new ones have already become lodged there. This unconscious mental process of digestion and assimilation I have several times experienced in my own case." Waldstein says: "The mind receives from experience certain data, and elaborates them unconsciously by laws peculiar to itself, and the result merges into consciousness." Holmes says: "Sir W. B. Hamilton discovered quaternions on 15th of October, 1843. On that day he was walking from his observatory at Dublin, with Lady Hamilton, when, on reaching the bridge, he 'felt the galvanic circle of thought close,' and the sparks that fell from it were the fundamental relations between *i. j. k.*, just as he used them ever afterwards.

Thompson said: "At times I have had a feeling of the uselessness of all voluntary effort, and also that the matter was working itself clear in my mind. It has many times seemed to me that I was really a passive instrument in the hands of a person not myself.

In view of having to wait for the results of these unconscious processes, I have proved the habit of getting together material in advance, and then leaving the mass to digest itself till I am ready to write about it. I delayed for a month the writing of my book, System of Psychology, but continued reading the authorities. I would not try to think about the book. I would watch with interest people passing the windows. One evening when reading the paper, the substance of the missing part of the book flashed upon my mind, and I began to write. This is only a sample of many such experiences…. In writing this work I have been unable to arrange my knowledge of a subject for days and weeks, until I experienced a clearing up of my mind, when I took my pen and unhesitatingly wrote the result. I have best accomplished this by leading the (conscious) mind as far away as possible from the subject upon which I was writing."

Mozart said: "I cannot really say that I can account for my compositions. My ideas flow, and I cannot say whence or how they come. I do not hear in my imagination the parts successively, but I hear them, as it were, all at once. The rest is merely an attempt to reproduce what I have heard." A writer has said of Berthelot, the great French chemist, and founder of Synthetic Chemistry: "He has told his intimates that the experiments which led to many of his wonderful discoveries were not the result of carefully followed trains of thought, or of pure reasoning processes, but on the contrary they 'came of themselves, so to speak,' as if from the clear sky above."

All investigators of the subconscious regions of the mind have been struck with the ease whereby the subconscious faculties may be trained to perform the drudgery of thought for their owner. By certain systems of autosuggestion the subconscious faculties may be commanded to thresh out difficult problems and then present the result to the field of consciousness. In a short time these faculties will become accustomed to the process, and will willingly and gladly perform their allotted tasks. Many men of affairs have unwittingly acquired this habit of "unconscious rumination" and much of their mental digestion is accomplished in this way, the result being that they are able to perform what seems like an incredible amount of mental work, but which really taxes their ordinary consciousness very little, and leaves them plenty of time for recreation, sport, etc.

Stevenson informed his intimate friends that he was indebted to his subconscious mentality in its phase of dreams, for many of the incidents and ideas contained in his charming books. He also wrote the following concerning the matter: "My Brownies! God bless them! who do one-half of my work for me when I am fast asleep, and in all human likelihood do the rest for me as well when I am wide awake and foolishly suppose that I do it for myself. I had long been wanting to write a book on man's double being. For two days I went about racking my brains for a plot of any sort and on the second night I dreamt the scene in Dr. Jekyll and Mr. Hyde at the window; and a scene, afterwards split in two, in which Hyde, pursued, took the powder and underwent the change in the presence of his pursuer. In Otalla, the Count, the mother, Otalla's chamber, the meeting on the stairs, the broken window, were all given me in bulk and details, as I have tried to write them."

Abercrombie says: "A distinguished lawyer had studied for days a most important case. One night his wife saw him rise up in the night, sit down, write a long paper which he put in his desk, and return to bed. Next morning, he told his wife he had a most interesting dream; that he had delivered a clear and luminous opinion on the case, and that he would give anything to recover the train of thought which had occurred. She then directed him to the writing desk, where he found all he had dreamt clearly and fully written out." Lord Kames once said: "There are various interesting operations of which we have no consciousness, and yet that they have existed is made known by their effects. Often have I gone to bed with a confused notion of what I was studying, and have awakened in the morning complete master of the subject." Schofield gives what he calls "a remarkable illustration of motor action in sleep that occurred to my niece of thirteen last summer. She had been practicing for days a 'shake' of great difficulty in a sonata, with very little success. One night her mother who slept with her was awakened by feeling fingers on her face. She asked her daughter what she was doing. But the child was in a profound sleep, while the fingers of her right hand were incessantly practicing the shake on her mother's face. Next day to the amazement of her mistress she could play it perfectly." Schofield says: "Coleridge is said to have dreamed 'Kubla Khan' after dinner during a nap, and wrote it down line by line when he awoke." Hudson mentions the same occurrence, giving it, however, a slightly different explanation, saying: "Many of the dreams of Coleridge furnish striking examples of the dominance of the subjective in poetry. His readers will readily recall the celebrated fragment entitled Kubla Kahn; or a Vision in a Dream, beginning as follows:

'In Xanadu did Kubla Khan

 A stately pleasure-dome decree—

Where Alph, the sacred river ran

Through caverns measureless to man

Down to a sunless sea.'

It is unfortunately true that the subjective condition in his case was brought about by artificial means; and it is expressly stated in a prefatory note to 'Kubla Khan' that this fragment was written under the influence of an anodyne. As an illustration of the principle under consideration it is, however, none the less valuable; while the career of the gifted but unfortunate poet should serve as a warning against the practices in which he indulged."

While the older schools of psychology clearly point out the possibilities of unconscious cerebration, as may be seen by reference to the quotations contained in this chapter, yet it has remained for The New Psychology to point out a way to turn these subconscious activities to advantage—a method whereby one might be able to start into activity the subconscious faculties of the mind and also direct them into certain particular channels. An understanding of the laws of suggestion in its phase of auto-suggestion will enable anyone to avail himself of the activities of the "brownies"—as Stevenson so happily styles the subconscious workings of the mind—which, "God bless them I do one-half of my work for me when I am fast asleep."

In the volume of this series, entitled "Suggestion and Auto-Suggestion" we have explained in detail the processes and methods which may be employed with success in the direction of turning to practical account these wonderful activities of the subconscious mind, instead of merely regarding them as curious phenomena of psychology. We cannot attempt to enter into this phase of the subject in this work, owing to the extent of its particular field, and as, moreover, to do so would be merely to repeat what we have said in the volume to which we have alluded. We have thought it proper, however, to mention the matter here, that those who are not familiar with the subject may be directed to a source from which they may receive practical instruction along these important lines.

5
A Remarkable Instance.

Among the celebrated instances of subconscious mentation found in the records of psychological research we find that of Zerah Colburn, the mathematical prodigy, whose feats were typically subconscious in their nature. This case is such a typical one, and brings out the characteristics of subconscious mentation so clearly, that we think it worthwhile to quote in full the report regarding it, taken from the *Annual Register* of 1812, a conservative English publication. The writer in the journal said:

"The attention of the philosophical world has been lately attracted by the most singular phenomenon in the history of human mind that perhaps ever existed. It is the case of a child, *under eight years of age*, who, without any previous knowledge of the common rules of arithmetic, or even of the use and powers of the Arabic numerals, and without having given any attention to the subject, possesses as if by intuition, the singular faculty of solving a great variety of arithmetical questions by the mere operation of the mind, and without the usual assistance of any visible symbol or contrivance. The name of the child is Zerah Colburn, who was born at Cabut (a town lying at the head of the Onion River in Vermont, in the United States of America) on the first of September, 1804. About two years ago,—August, 1810,— although at that time *not six years of age*, he first began to show these wonderful powers of calculation which have since so much attracted the attention, and excited the astonishment of every person who has witnessed his extraordinary abilities. The discovery was made by accident. His father, who had not given him any other instruction than such as was to be obtained at a small school established in that unfrequented and remote part of the country, and which did not include either writing or ciphering, was much surprised one day to hear him repeating the products of several numbers. Struck with amazement at the circumstance, he proposed a variety of arithmetical questions to him, all of which the child solved with remarkable facility and correctness. The news of the infant prodigy was soon circulated through the neighborhood, and many persons came from distant parts to witness so singular a circumstance. The father, encouraged by the unanimous opinion of all who came to see him, was induced to undertake with this child the tour of the United States. They were everywhere received with the most flattering expressions, and in several towns which they visited, various plans were suggested to educate and bring up the child free from all expense to his family. Yielding, however, to the pressing solicitations of his friends, and urged by the most respectable and powerful recommendations, as well as by a view to his son's more complete education, the father has brought the child to this country (England), where they arrived on the 12th of May last; and the inhabitants of this metropolis (London) have for the last three months had an opportunity of seeing and examining this wonderful phenomenon, and verifying the reports that have been circulated regarding him. Many persons of the first eminence for the knowledge in mathematics, and well known for their philosophical inquiries, have made a point of seeing and conversing with him, and they have all been struck with astonishment at his extraordinary powers.

"It is correctly true, as stated of him, that he will not only determine with the greatest facility and dispatch the exact number of seconds or minutes in any given period of time, but will also solve any other question of a similar kind. He will tell the exact product arising from the multiplication of any number consisting of two, three or four figures by any other number consisting of the like number of figures. Or, any number consisting of six or seven places of figures being proposed, he will determine with equal expedition and ease all the factors of which it is composed. This singular faculty consequently extends not only to the raising of powers, but to the extraction of the square and cube roots of the number proposed, and likewise to the means of determining whether it is a prime number (or a number incapable of division by any other number); for which case there does not exist at present any general rule among mathematicians. All these and a variety of other questions connected therewith are answered by this child with such promptness and accuracy (and in the midst of his juvenile pursuits) as to astonish every person who has visited him.

"At a meeting of his friends, which was held for the purpose of concerting the best methods of promoting the views of the father, the child undertook and completely succeeded in raising the number 8 progressively up to the sixteenth power. And, in naming the last result; viz., 281,474,976,710,656! he was right in every figure. He was then tried as to other numbers consisting of one figure, all of which he raised (by actual multiplication, and not by memory) as high as the tenth power, with so much facility and dispatch that the person appointed to take down the results was obliged to enjoin him not to be so rapid. With respect to numbers consisting of two figures, he would raise some of them to the sixth, seventh and eighth powers, but not always with equal facility; for the larger the products became, the more difficult he found it to proceed. He was asked the square root of 106,929; and before the number could be written down, he immediately answered, "327." He was then required to name the cube root of 268,336,125; and with equal facility and promptness he replied, "645." Various other questions of a similar nature, respecting the roots and powers of very high numbers, were proposed by several of the gentlemen present, to all of which he answered in a similar manner. One of the party requested him to name the factors which produced the number 247,483; this he immediately did by mentioning the numbers 941 and 263,—which, indeed, are the only two numbers that will produce it.

Another of them proposed 171,395, and he named the following factors as the only ones; viz., 5×34,279, 7×24,485, 59×2,905, 83×2,065, 35×4,897, 295×581, and 413×415. He was then asked to give the factors of 36,083; but he immediately replied that it had none,—which in fact was the case, as 36,083 is a prime number. Other numbers were indiscriminately proposed to him, and he always succeeded in giving the correct factors, except in the case of prime numbers, which he discovered almost as soon as proposed.

"One of the gentlemen asked him how many minutes there were in forty-eight years; and before the question could be written down he replied, 25,228,800; and instantly added that the number of seconds in the same period was 1,513,728,000. Various questions of the like kind were put to him, and to all of them he answered with equal facility and promptitude, so as to astonish every one present, and to excite a desire that so extraordinary a faculty should, if possible, be rendered more extensive and useful. It was the wish of the gentlemen present to obtain a knowledge of the method by which the child was enabled to answer with so much facility and correctness the questions thus put to him; but to all their inquiries on the subject (and he was closely examined on this point) he was unable to give them any information. He persistently declared— and every observation that was made seemed to justify the assertion—

that he did not know how the answer came into his mind. In the act of multiplying two numbers together, and in the raising of powers, it was evident, not only from the motion of his lips, but also from some singular facts which will be hereafter mentioned, that some operations were going forward in his mind; and yet that operation could not, from the readiness with which the answers were furnished, be at all allied to the usual mode of proceeding with such subjects; and moreover he is entirely ignorant of the common rules of arithmetic, and cannot perform upon paper a simple sum in multiplication or division. But in the extraction of roots and in mentioning the factors of high numbers, it does not appear that any operation can take place, since he will give the answer immediately, or in a very few seconds, where it would require, according to the ordinary method of solution, a very difficult or laborious calculation; and moreover, the knowledge of a prime number cannot be obtained by any known rule.

"It must be evident, from what has here been stated, that the singular faculty which this child possesses is not altogether dependent on his memory. In the multiplication of numbers and in the raising of powers, he is doubtless considerably assisted by that remarkable quality of the mind; and in this respect he might be considered as bearing some resemblance (if the difference of age did not prevent the justness of the comparison) to the celebrated Jedidiah Buxton, and other persons of similar note. But in the extraction of roots of numbers and in determining their factors, if any, it is clear to all those who have witnessed the astonishing quickness and accuracy of this child that the memory has nothing to do with the process. And in this particular point consists the remarkable difference between the present and all former instances of an apparently similar kind."

It is interesting to note the sequel to the above account.

The child was placed in schools and was given the regular education in mathematics. It was believed that in this way his mental process might be systematized and that he would be able to establish a new method of making mental calculations, which would be of great benefit to the race. But, as in all of such cases, his remarkable power decreased as he was educated in the ordinary methods of mathematics, and finally it left him almost entirely and he became no more than the ordinary trained student. The door to the inner chamber closed, and he was compelled to perform his calculations in the ordinary manner.

6
The Subconscious Memory.

Memory was formerly regarded as a special faculty of the mind, but the later psychologists have agreed that Memory, instead of being a faculty is a manifestation of subconscious mental activity and power. Just what Memory *is* psychology is unable to inform us, but that it belongs to the phenomena of the subconscious region of the mind there is no longer any doubt. In some way the subconscious mind stores away the impressions received through the senses so that they may be revived in response to certain stimulating influences. Kay says: "It is impossible to understand the true nature of memory, or to train it aright, unless we have a clear conception of the fact that there is much in the mind of which we are unconscious."

It was formerly thought that only certain impressions were retained in the memory, the remainder being dissipated and lost. But the later thought on the subject leads us to the conclusion that anything and everything impressed upon the mind remains in the subconscious storehouse of the memory ready to be recalled under the proper stimulus. Many impressions are never recalled, the stimulus being lacking; but there is every reason to suppose that they remain registered in the mind, nevertheless. Kay says: "There is every reason to believe that the changes which result...are not evanescent; that they do not vanish away as soon as the causes by which they were produced have passed away; but that, on the contrary, they remain and form a permanent record of what has passed through the mind—a written testimony of all that one has been, felt and done in the past.... In this way we believe that every good or evil thought we have ever entertained, every good or evil act that we have ever done, is indelibly recorded in our bodily structure, to be brought back to mind, if not in this life, at least on the Great Day of Account, when our bodies will be raised and the deeds of all men made manifest.... We have already expressed the opinion that every impression we receive, every thought we think, as well as every action we do, causes some change in the material structure of our bodies, and that this change is permanent, forming an imperishable record of all that we have experienced, thought, or done in the past. In like manner we believe that every impression or thought that has once been before consciousness remains ever after impressed in the mind. It may never again come up before consciousness, but it will doubtless remain in that vast ultra-conscious region of the mind, unconsciously moulding and fashioning our subsequent thoughts and actions."

Morrell says: "We have every reason to believe that mental power once called forth follows the analogy of everything we see in the material universe in the fact of its perpetuity.... Every single effort of mind is a creation which can never go back again into nonentity. It may slumber in the depths of forgetfulness as light and heat slumber in the coal seams, but there it is, ready at the bidding of some appropriate stimulus to come again out of the darkness into the light of consciousness." Benecke says:

"Every impression we receive leaves a trace, a real physiological trace behind it, which may be revived and brought again into consciousness under the proper physical conditions." McCrie says: "No sensation received, no judgment formed, no acquisition made, no affection cherished, no passion gratified, will ever be found to have faded into nothing, as if they had never been.... Deem not this to be impossible. In the case of drowning, those who have been preserved and recover declare that the whole of their past lives did at that moment pass before them with the velocity of lightning."

Kay says: "It is only a small part of what exists in the mind that we are at any time conscious of. There is always much that is known to be in the mind that exists in it unconsciously, and must be stored away somewhere. We may be able to recall it into consciousness when we wish to do so, but at other times the mind is unconscious of its existence. Further, everyone's experience must tell him that there is much in his mind that he cannot always recall when he may wish to do so,—much that he can recover only after a labored search, or that he may search for in vain at the time, but which may occur to him afterwards when perhaps he is not thinking of it. Again, much that we probably would never be able to recall, or that would not recur to us under ordinary circumstances, we may remember to have had in mind when it is mentioned to us by others. In such a case there must still have remained some trace or scintilla of it in the mind before we could recognize it as having been there before. These cases occur in ordinary states of the mind, but in abnormal or exalted mental conditions we find still more remarkable instances. Thus in somnambulism, dreams, hysteria, the delirium of fever, or on the approach of death, persons have been known to recall events of their past life, long since forgotten, and unable to be recalled under ordinary circumstances. Persons in a delirium of fever have been known to speak in a language which they had known in their childhood, but which for many years had passed from their memory; or to repeat with apparent accuracy discourses to which they had listened many years previously, but of which before the fever they had no recollection. They have even been known to repeat accurately long passages from books in foreign tongues, of which they never had any understanding, and had no recollection of in health, but which they had casually heard recited many years before. The most remarkable cases, however, are those of persona who have been resuscitated from drowning or hanging, and who have reported that they had a sudden revelation of all the events of their past life presented to them with the utmost minuteness and distinctness just before consciousness left them."

Sir William Hamilton says: "The mind frequently contains whole systems of knowledge which, though in our normal state they have faded into absolute oblivion, may in certain abnormal states, as madness, febrile delirium, somnambulism, catalepsy, etc., flash out into luminous consciousness, and even throw into the shade of unconsciousness those other systems by which they had for a long period been eclipsed and even extinguished. For example, there are cases in which the extinct memory of whole languages was suddenly restored, and what is even still more remarkable, in which the faculty was exhibited of accurately repeating in known or unknown tongues passages which were never in the grasp of conscious memory in the normal state." Lecky says: "It is now fully established that a multitude of events which are so completely forgotten that no effort of the will can revive them, and that the statement of them calls up no reminiscences, may be nevertheless, so to speak, embedded in the memory, and may be reproduced with intense vividness under certain physical conditions." Beaufort, who once was rescued from drowning, afterward described his sensations at the time, saying: "Every incident of my former life seemed to glance across my recollection in a retrograde succession, not in mere outline, but the picture being filled with every minute and collateral feature, forming a kind of panoramic view of my entire existence, each act of it being accompanied by a sense of right or wrong."

As Kay says: "There is indeed every reason to believe that there is no such thing with any of us as absolutely forgetting anything that has once been in the mind." Schmid says: "All mental activities, all acts of knowledge which have once excited persist. We never wholly lose them, but they may become obscure.

The obscure cognition may exist simply out of consciousness, so that it can be recalled by a common act of reminiscence. Again it may be impossible to recover it by an act of voluntary recollection; but some association may revivify it enough to make it flash into consciousness after a long oblivion. Further it may be obscured so far that it can only be resuscitated by some morbid affection of the system; or, finally, it may be absolutely lost to us in this life, and destined only for our reminiscence in the life to come."

Kay says: "By adopting the opinion that every thought or impression that had once been consciously before the mind is ever afterward retained we obtain light on many obscure mental phenomena; and especially do we draw from it the conclusion of the perfectibility of the memory to an almost unlimited extent. We cannot doubt that, could we penetrate to the lowest depths of our mental nature, we should there find traces of every impression we have received, every thought we have entertained, and every act we have done throughout our past life, each one making its influence felt in the way of building up our present knowledge, or in guiding our every-day actions; and if they exist in the mind, might it not be possible to recall most if not all of them into consciousness when we wished to do so, if our memories or powers of recollection were what they should be."

Bowen says: "Many educated persons know four languages.

This will give 160,000 words, or 40,000 for each, which is an underestimate. These words are as arbitrary symbols as signs in algebra. Then consider the countless facts and ideas bound up with these words in a well-informed mind. Such a mind is far more richly stocked with words and ideas than the British Museum is with books. The British Museum will produce, after a hunt in catalogs and on shelves of perhaps ten minutes, any book wanted. But the single unconscious librarian who waits our orders in the crowded chambers of our memory is far more speedy and skillful in his service. A student reads a page of French or German in a minute, and for each of the 200 or 300 groups of hieroglyphics printed on it, the unconscious instantly furnishes us with whatever we call for; its meaning, its etymology, its English equivalent, or any associated ideas connected with it. We have no conscious clue to direct the search. It is enough we want the point to be remembered, and instantly it is produced out of the vast repository. I think this single illustration sufficient proof of the presence and agency of the unconscious. For what mechanical or chemical action is conceivable as a possible explanation of the phenomenon in question?"

A consideration of the facts brought out in the above quotations should serve to convince anyone that that which we ordinarily mean when we use the term Memory is but the art or faculty of *recollecting* or bringing forth that which is stored in the Memory. Likewise, memory is seen to be a characteristic quality of that great subconscious storehouse of the mind which is a phase of that which we call The Subconscious. It would then follow that The Subconscious *remembers everything and forgets nothing*. This being so, it will be evident that if we can manage to set the Subconscious to work out our mental problems for us, we may multiply our powers of mentation to a wonderful extent. Memory is stored-up knowledge—therefore he who has free access to that stored-up knowledge is far ahead of the average member of the race.

7
Typical Cases.

Dr. Hudson has said: "One of the most striking and important peculiarities of the subjective mind, as distinguished from the objective, consists in its prodigious memory. It would perhaps be hazardous to say that the memory of the subjective mind is perfect, but there is good ground for believing that such a proposition would be substantially true." Dr. Hudson seems to have regarded Memory as a quality possessed by both the objective and subjective minds, in different degrees, but later authorities hold that memory is essentially a quality or phase of the subconscious mind, and that the so-called "objective mind" or plane of ordinary consciousness does *not* possess memory and is merely conscious of what the subconscious memory brings into the field of consciousness. The following typical cases, related on good authority, and quoted by the best writers on the subject, will serve to bring out the peculiar and wonderful operation of the subconscious mind in its phase of memory.

Dr. Benjamin Bush, an eminent American surgeon, has recorded the following cases: "The records of the wit and cunning of madmen are numerous in every country. Talents for eloquence, poetry, music, and painting, and uncommon ingenuity in several of the mechanical arts, are often evolved in this state of madness. A gentleman whom I attended in a hospital, in the year 1810, often delighted as well as astonished the patients and officers of our hospital by his displays of oratory in preaching from a table in the hospital yard every Sunday. A female patient of mine who became insane, after parturition, in the year 1807, sang hymns and songs of her own composition during the latter stage of her illness, with a tone of voice so soft and pleasant that I hung upon it with delight every time I visited her. She had never discovered a talent for poetry or music in any previous part of her life. Two instances of a talent for drawing, evolved by madness, have occurred within my knowledge. And where is the hospital for mad people in which elegant and completely-rigged ships and curious pieces of machinery have not been exhibited by persons who never discovered the least turn for mechanical art previous to their derangement? Sometimes we observe in mad people an unexpected resuscitation of knowledge; hence we hear them describe past events, and speak in ancient or modern languages, or repeat long and interesting passages from books, none of which, we are sure, they were capable of recollecting in the natural and healthy state of their minds. In these cases, and many similar to them, the activities of the ordinary plane of consciousness are impaired or distorted, which seemingly results in allowing the subconscious activities to manifest more freely and with less restraint."

Sir William Hamilton quotes from the memoirs of an American clergyman named Flint, who stated: "I am aware that every sufferer in this way is apt to think his own case extraordinary. My physicians agreed with all who saw me that my case was so. As very few live to record the issue of a sickness like mine,...I will relate some of the circumstances of this disease. And it is in my view desirable...that more of the symptoms, sensations and sufferings should have been recorded than have been; and that others in similar predicaments may know that some before them have had sufferings like theirs, and have survived them. I had a fever before, and had risen, and been dressed every day. But in this, with the first day, I was prostrated to infantine weakness, and felt, with its first attack, that it was a thing very different from what I had yet experienced. Paroxysms of derangement occurred on the third day, and this was to me a new state of mind. That state of disease in which partial derangement is mixed with a consciousness generally sound, and sensibility preternaturally excited, I should suppose the most distressing of all its forms. At the same time that I was unable to recognize my friends, I was informed that my memory was more than ordinarily exact and retentive, and that I repeated whole passages in the different languages which I knew with entire accuracy. I recited, without losing or misplacing a word, a passage of poetry which I could not so repeat after I recovered my health."

Monboddo reports the following case, related to him by a friend of excellent standing. The friend states the case in these words: "About six-and-twenty years ago, when I was in France, I had an intimacy in the family of the late Marechal de Monmorenci de Laval. His son, the Comte de Laval, was married to Mademoiselle de Manpeaux, the daughter of a lieutenant of that name, and the niece of the late chancellor. This

33

gentleman was killed at the battle of Hastenbeck. His widow survived him some years but is since dead. The following fact comes from her own mouth; she has told it me repeatedly. She was a woman of perfect veracity and very good sense. She appealed to her servants and family for the truth. Nor did she, indeed seem to be sensible that the matter was so extraordinary as it appeared to me. I wrote it down at the time, and I have the memorandum among some of my papers. The Comtesse de Laval had been observed, by servants who sat up with her on account of some indisposition, to talk in her sleep a language that none of them understood; nor were they sure, or, indeed, herself able to guess, upon the sounds being repeated to her, whether it was or was not gibberish. Upon her lying-in of one of her children, she was attended by a nurse who was of the province of Brittany, and who immediately knew the meaning of what she had said, it being in the idiom of the natives of that country; but she herself when awake did not understand a single syllable of what she had uttered in her sleep, upon it being retold her. She was born in that province, and had been nursed in a family where nothing but that language was spoken; so that in her infancy she had known it, and no other; but when she returned to her parents, she had no opportunity of keeping up the use of it; and as I have before said, she did not understand a word of Breton when awake, though she spoke it in her sleep. I need not say that the Comtesse de Laval never said or imagined that she used any words of the Breton idiom, more than was necessary to express those ideas that are within the compass of a child's knowledge of objects."

Coleridge relates the following interesting case, which has been widely quoted by later writers: "It occurred in a Roman Catholic town in Germany, a year or two before my arrival at Gottingen, and had not then ceased to be a frequent subject for conversation. A young woman of four or five and twenty, who could neither read nor write, was seized with a nervous fever, during which, according to the asseverations of all the priests and monks of the neighborhood, she became possessed; and, as it appeared, by a very learned devil. She continued incessantly talking Latin, Greek and Hebrew, in very pompous tones, and with most distinct enunciation. This possession was rendered more probable by the known fact that she was, or had been, a heretic. Voltaire humorously advises the devil to decline all acquaintance with medical men; and it would have been more to his reputation if he had taken this advice in the present instance. The case had attracted the particular attention of a young physician, and by his statement many eminent physiologists and psychologists visited the town and cross-examined the case on the spot. Sheets full of her ravings were take down from her own mouth, and were found to consist of sentences, coherent and intelligible each for itself, but with little or no connection with each other. Of the Hebrew, a small portion only could be traced to the Bible; the remainder seemed to be in the Rabbinical dialect. All trick or conspiracy was out of the question. Not only had the young woman ever been a harmless, simple creature, but she was evidently laboring under a nervous fever. In a town in which she had been a resident for many years as a servant in different families, no solution presented itself.

"The young physician, however, determined to trace her past life step by step; for the patient herself was incapable of returning a rational answer. He at length succeeded in discovering the place where her parents had lived; traveled thither, found them dead, but an uncle surviving; and from him learned that the patient had been charitably taken by an old Protestant pastor at nine years old, and had remained with him some years, even till the old man's death. Of this pastor the uncle knew nothing, but that he was a very good man. With great difficulty, and after much search, our young medical philosopher discovered a niece of the pastor's who had lived with him as his housekeeper, and had inherited his effects. She remembered the girl; related that her venerable uncle had been too indulgent, and could not bear to hear the girl scolded; that she was willing to have kept her, but that, after her parent's death, the girl herself refused to stay. Anxious inquiries were then, of course, made concerning the pastor's habits; and the solution of the phenomenon was soon obtained. For it appeared that it had been the old man's custom for years to walk up and down a passage of his house into which the kitchen-door opened, and to read to himself, with a loud voice, out of his favorite books. A considerable number of these were still in the niece's possession. She added that he was a very learned man and a great Hebraist. Among the books were found a collection of Rabbinical writings, together with several of the Greek and Latin Fathers; and the physician succeeded in identifying so many passages with those taken down at the young woman's bedside, that no doubt could remain in any rational mind concerning the true origin of the impressions made on her nervous system."

8
Inherited Memory.

Memory is a far greater thing than is generally imagined. Not only does it include the storing away and retention of impressions received by the individual, but also the retention of impressions received, and experiences gathered, by the ancestors of the individual. There are certain race memories stored away in the great subconscious region of the mind which have much to do with our thoughts, feelings and actions. So little is this recognized that many will dispute the statement when they first hear it. But a little consideration will show anyone that all that we call "inherited tendencies and tastes; instinct," is but a form of memory transmitted from one organism to another along the lines of heredity. Our ancestors live in and through us, though they have long passed away from the scene of earthly life.

What we call "instinct" gives us a very good idea of this form of memory. James says: "Instinct is usually defined as the faculty of acting in such a way as to produce certain ends, without foresight of the ends, and without previous education in the performance." Halleck says: "Instinct gives complex action toward a definite end which is not foreseen, as when the silkworm spins her shroud.... When a conscious sensation, due either to external or internal stimuli, results in purpositive action toward a given end which is not foreseen, that action is instinctive. A young stork left alone in a northern latitude would migrate southward on the approach of autumn.... If the bird had never been south before, he could have no idea of the purpose of his flight although it would be action directed toward an intelligent end. Certain sensations of organic origin prompt the young bird to build its first nest. This bird has never been taught, nor has it had any experience of nest-building. Yet the first nest is constructed on the same principles and fashioned as well as any of its successors. All the actions—the spreading of the wings in light, the gathering of grass, straw and twigs, the moistening of the bill for making mud—are a series of complex movements blindly directed toward an intelligent end.... When the caterpillar feels certain stimuli, it mechanically begins to weave a shroud in a blind, reflex way, and the action is continued so long as the stimuli are operative. If a stork is confined in a cage with iron bars, so strong as to shut off hope of escape, when the stimulus of autumnal cold affects the bird, it will repeatedly dash its breast against the bars until it is bloody...Darwin says that young salmon kept in a tub of water will often leap out at a certain time, and thus commit unintentional suicide."

James says: "The cat runs after the mouse, runs or shows fight before the dog, avoids falling from walls and trees, shuns fire and water, not because he has any notion either of life or of death, or of self-preservation...He acts in each case separately, and simply because he cannot help it; being so framed that when that particular running thing called a mouse appears in his field of vision he *must* pursue; that when that particular barking and obstreperous thing called a dog appears there he *must* retire, if at a distance, and scratch if close by; that he *must* withdraw his feet from water and his face from flame, etc.... Now, why do the various animals do what seem to us such strange things, in the presence of such outlandish stimuli? Why does the hen, for example, submit herself to the tedium of incubating such a fearfully uninteresting set of objects as a nestful of eggs, unless she have some sort of a prophetic inkling of the result? The only answer is *ad hominem*. We can only interpret the instinct of brutes by what we know of instincts in ourselves. Why do men always lie down, when they can, on soft beds rather than on hard floors? Why do they sit around a stove on a cold day? Why, in a room, do they place themselves, ninety-nine times out a hundred, with their faces toward its middle rather than to the wall?... Why does the maiden interest the youth so much that everything about her seems more important and significant than anything else in the world? Nothing more can be said than that these are human ways, and that every creature *likes* its own ways, and takes to following them as a matter of course. Science may come and consider these ways, and find that most of them are useful. But it is not for the sake of their utility that they are followed, but because at the moment of following them we feel that that is the only appropriate and natural thing to do. Not one man in a million, when taking his dinner, ever thinks of its utility. He eats because the food tastes good, and makes him want more. If you should ask him *why* he should want to eat more of what tastes like that, instead of revering you as a philosopher he will probably laugh at you for a fool.... It takes, in short, what Berkeley calls a mind debauched by learning to carry the process of making the natural seem strange, so far as to ask for the *why* of any instinctive human act. To the metaphysician alone can such questions occur as: Why do we smile, when pleased, and not scowl? Why are we unable to talk to a crowd as to a single friend? Why does a particular maiden turn our wits upside down? The common man can only say—'*Of course* we smile, *of course* our heart palpitates at the sight of the crowd, *of course* we love the maiden,— that beautiful soul clad in that perfect form, so palpably and flagrantly made from all eternity to be loved!' And so, probably, does each animal feel about the particular things it tends to do in the presence of particular objects. They, too, are *a priori* syntheses. To the lion it is the lioness which is made to be loved; to the bear, the she-bear. To the broody hen the notion would seem monstrous that there should be a creature in the world to whom a nestful of eggs was not the utterly fascinating, precious and never-to-be-too-much-sat-upon object which it is to her. Thus we may be sure that however mysterious some animals' instincts may appear to us, our instincts will appear no less mysterious to them. And we may conclude that, to the animal which obeys it, every impulse and every step of every instinct shines with its own sufficient light, and seems at the moment the only externally right and proper thing to do. It may be done for its own sake exclusively. What voluptuous thrill may not shake a fly, when she at last discovers the one particular leaf, or carrion, or bit of dung, that out of all the world can stimulate her ovipositor to its discharge? Does not the discharge then seem to her the only fitting thing? And need she care or know anything about the future maggot and its food?"

James also says: "Nothing is commoner than the remark that man differs from lower creatures by the almost total absence of instincts, and the assumption of their work in him by reason.... We may confidently say that however uncertain man's reactions upon his environment may sometimes seem in comparison with those of the lower mammals, the uncertainty is probably not due to their possession of any principles of action which he lacks. *On the contrary, man possesses all the impulses that they have, and a great many more besides.*

Schneider says: "It is a fact that men, especially in childhood, fear to go into a dark cavern, or a gloomy wood. This feeling of fear arises, to be sure, partly from the fact that we easily suspect that dangerous beasts may lurk in these localities—a suspicion due to stories we have beard and read. But, on the other hand, it is quite sure that this fear at a certain perception is also directly inherited. Children who have been carefully guarded from all ghost stories are nevertheless terrified and cry if led into a dark place, especially if sounds are made there. Even an adult can easily observe that an uncomfortable timidity steals over him in a lonely wood at night, although he may have the fixed conviction that not the slightest danger is near. This feeling of fear occurs in many men even in their own house after dark, although it is much stronger in a dark cavern or forest. The fact of such instinctive fear is easily explicable when we consider that our savage ancestors through innumerable generations were accustomed to meet with dangerous beasts in caverns, especially bears, and were for the most part attacked by such beasts during the night and in the woods, and that thus an inseparable association between the perceptions of darkness, caverns, woods, and fear took place, and was inherited."

James says: "High places cause fear of a peculiarly sickening sort, though, here again, individuals differ greatly. The utterly blind instinctive character of the motor impulses here is shown by the fact that they are almost always entirely unreasonable, but that reason is powerless to suppress them...Certain ideas of supernatural agency, associated with real circumstances, produce a peculiar kind of horror. This horror is probably explicable as the result of a combination of simple horrors. To bring the ghostly terror to its maximum, many usual elements of the dreadful must combine, such as loneliness, darkness, inexplicable sounds, especially of a dismal character, moving figures half discerned (or, if discerned, of dreadful aspect), and a vertiginous baffling of the expectation.... In view of the fact that cadaveric, reptilian, and underground horrors play so specific and constant a part in many nightmares and forms of delirium, it seems not altogether unwise to ask whether these forms of dreadful circumstance may not at a former period have been more normal objects of the environment than now. The...evolutionist ought to have no difficulty in explaining these terrors, and the scenery that provokes them, as relapses into the consciousness of the cave-men, a consciousness usually overlaid in us by experiences of a more recent date.... There are certain other pathological fears, and certain peculiarities in the expression of ordinary fear, which may receive an explanatory light from ancestral conditions, even infra-human ones. In ordinary fear one may either run, or remain semi-paralyzed. The latter condition reminds us of the so-called death-shamming instinct as shown by many animals.... It is simply a terror-paralysis which has become so useful as to become hereditary...Again, take the strange symptom which has been described of late years by the rather absurd name of *agoraphobia*. The patient is seized with palpitation and terror at the sight of any open place or broad street which he has to cross alone. He trembles, his knees bend, he may even faint at the idea. Where he has sufficient self-command he sometimes accomplishes the object by keeping safe under the lee of a vehicle going across or joining himself to a knot of other people. But usually he slinks round the sides of the square, hugging the houses as closely as he can. This emotion has no utility in a civilized man, but when we notice the chronic *agoraphobia* of our domestic cats, and see the tenacious way in which many wild animals, especially rodents, cling to cover, and only venture on a dash across the open as a desperate measure—even then making for every stone or bunch of weeds which may give a momentary shelter—when we see this we are strongly tempted to ask whether such an odd kind of fear in us is not due to the accidental resurrection, through disease, of a sort of instinct which may in some of our remote ancestors have had a permanent and on the whole a useful part to play!"

Clodd says: "Instinct is the higher form of reflex action. The salmon migrates from sea to river; the bird makes its nest or migrates from one zone to another by an unvarying route, even leaving its young behind to perish; the bee builds its six-sided cell; the spider spins its web; the chick breaks its way through the shell, balances itself, and picks up grains of corn; the new-born babe sucks its mother's breast—all in virtue of like acts on the part of their ancestors, which, arising in the needs of the creature, and gradually, becoming automatic, have not varied during long ages, the tendency to repeat them being transmitted within the germ from which insect, fish, bird, and man have severally sprung.... Even the so-called necessary truths and innate ideas of the mind, as of time and space, take their place among transmitted experiences. 'Being,' as Herbert Spencer says, 'the constant and infinitely repeated elements of thought, they must become the automatic elements of thought of which it is impossible to get rid.... An interesting illustration is supplied by a St. Bernard dog belonging to a relative. The dog was born in London, and taken into the country when a puppy. After a few months a sharp fall of snow happened, and 'Ju' who had never seen snow before, was frantic to get outdoors. When she was free, she rolled in the snow, and dug it up with her claws as if rescuing some belated traveler. The same excitement was shown whenever snow fell."

The student of the subject of Instinct soon discovers that the entire phenomena is bound up with the idea of Memory— instinct is by transmitted memory. And memory is essentially a function of the subconscious plane of mind. Therefore all that is included in the general field of Instinct really forms a part of the phenomena of the subconscious.

The "feeling" phase of man's mental nature is largely composed of inherited memories of the past experiences of the race. As Burbank says: "Heredity means much, but what is heredity?

Not some hideous ancestral spectre, forever crossing the path of a human being. Heredity is simply *the sum of all the effects of all the environments of all past generations* on the responsive ever-moving life forces." The individual inherits very little *from* his own parents or grandparents, but very much *through* them. For through them flows the life-stream of countless generations of men, the combined experiences of whom have left a subtle mental essence which is transmitted to the race. Many of man's emotions, feelings, tastes and inclinations, are the result of these race experiences of the past. There is much of the cave-man even in the most cultured individual, which comes to the surface when opportunity presents itself and environment supplies the stimulus. Civilization is only skin-deep—culture is only superficial. Beneath the thin veneer of our civilization lies the great mass of the race experience with all its primitive emotions, tendencies and impulses.

Not only in a general way do these race experiences, the memory of which is preserved in the subconscious mind, affect the individual. Here and there, upon occasions, flashes of recollection pass before the mind of the individual, often startling him with their suggestions of a knowledge of things known by some ancestral mind in the early days of the race. Certain scenes, certain surroundings, certain happenings, awaken into activity traces of the memory of the past, and the individual is filled with a sense of familiarity at the scene, the happening, or the surrounding circumstances. Science informs us that many of the dreams of the race, especially the nightmares, are the result of the reawakening of subconscious memories of the past experiences of ancestors of perhaps several thousand years ago. The frightful monsters of the nightmare are by recollections of the prehistoric animals which terrified the minds of the cave-man ancestor. The familiar dream of running about clad only in the scantiest raiment, or else utterly devoid of clothing, and yet feeling no sense of shame—only to be overcome with shame and confusion as we awaken—are held to be traces of ancestral memories. The familiar dream of falling from a high place is held to be a race-memory of ancestors who fell from trees or over the precipices of their cave-dwellings.

The peculiarity of this last dream is that the dreamer always is awakened before he reaches the bottom of the cliff, or the foot of the tree. The ancestor who failed to have his fall arrested did not live to transmit his experience!

Jack London in his interesting story *Before Adam* brings out this point very clearly, and his hero tells of his unusual dreams in which the entire life of one of his cave-dwelling ancestors is reproduced clearly. There seems to be good reason for believing that much that we call "intuitive knowledge" is but a well-developed faculty of recollecting the experiences of the race, treasured up in our subconsciousness. Scientists have calculated that each of us of course has thousands of ancestors, and that frequent crossing of the ancestral lines has occurred, so that practically every individual living to-day has among his ancestors *every individual* of the race who lived five thousand years ago. So the ancestry of the race is practically common to all, hence the uniformity of the more elementary feelings and tendencies of the race. Each and every individual is an heir to *all* the experiences of past generations.

Without attempting to enter into a discussion of the subject of reincarnation, we may say that the majority of instances advanced in favor of the theory, in which traces of memories of the past form a part, may be equally well-accounted for upon the theory of racial memory. Not only is this true regarding the elementary impressions of race thought, but also of specific instances in which the individual has a distinct recollection of having experienced certain things before, or having witnessed certain scenes before. There are a number of well-authenticated cases on record in which persons having these experiences have, upon investigation, found that some near ancestor had undergone similar experiences, or had visited the scenes in question. One particular case relates the experience of a young man who visited a small place in England, and stopped at an old inn. The moment he entered the room he was overcome by the sense of familiarity with the surroundings. He seemed to have a clear recollection of having been in the same room before— many years before. He stated his impressions to a friend who was with him, and finally said, "If I have ever been here before, I then wrote my name with a diamond on the lowest window-pane of that left-hand window." They approached the window, and there in the corner of the pane was a name scratched with a diamond, as the young man had stated. But it was not *his* name, but the name of his grandfather, accompanied by a date showing it to have been written there when the latter was a young man.

Another case was that of a young woman who saw as if in a vision (although wide-awake at the time) a picture of herself accompanied by a young man, the latter carving a heart on the smooth bark of an old tree, and placing two sets of initials within it. She had never been in the place before, although it was the home of a distant relation. An examination of the tree showed the faint trace of a heart containing the initials of her father and her mother, the latter being the initials of her mother's maiden name. Inquiry from old relatives revealed the fact, unknown to the girl, that her father had courted her mother in that very park adjoining the house of the relative, many years before. We have heard of the case of a young woman who found an old packet of letters belonging to her grandmother, and who knew, and told others, of their contents, before she untied them. She said that she felt as if she herself had received the letters many years before. On several occasions, we have heard young women say that they "felt like" their mother, or grandmother, as the case happened to be. They were not able to describe just what were their sensations, but tried to explain that their sense of identity seemed to merge with that of the mother, or grandmother.

There are doubtless many instances of this kind known to persons who may lead these lines, all of which would seem to establish the existence of distinct inherited memories, transmitted from ancestor to descendent. And this would be but any set of facts concerning the phenomena of the subconscious plane of mind, for such impressions and memories could reside only in that region of the mind. The subconscious is the storehouse of all that has gone before, both individual experiences and those of the race.

9
Mental Habit.

Among the many phases of the subconscious we find the phenomena of Mental Habit. Mental Habit belongs to the subconscious plane of mentation, for the reason that its activities are performed below the ordinary plane of consciousness. That which was originally performed on the conscious plane is afterward passed on to the subconscious plane and becomes akin to the activities of Instinct. In fact many of the actions performed by the average person are strictly instinctive—almost as much so as are the actions resulting from inherited or transmitted instinct.

Instinct is but inherited habit. Habit is but acquired instinct. Mental habit is analogous to certain tendencies of inanimate things. As Dumont has well said: "Every one knows how a garment, after having been worn a certain time, clings to the shape of the body better than when it was new; there has been a change in the tissue, and this change is a new habit of cohesion. A lock works better after being used some time; at the outset more force was required to overcome certain roughness in the mechanism. The overcoming of their resistance is a phenomena of habituation. It costs less trouble to fold a paper when it has been folded already;...and just so in the nervous system the impressions of outer objects fashion for themselves more and more appropriate paths, and these vital phenomena recur under similar excitements from without, when they have been interrupted a certain time."

Schofield says: "Do we not see in an old dress, even in a room, a something that speaks of habit, an adaptability of shape and crease from constant wearing and use, or of fittings and furniture, that cannot be seen in a new coat or lodgings? Does not an old violin that has been the property of some great master (not only made by some great maker) retain in its very fibres the habit of responding to the grand chords he struck, with far greater ease than any instrument that had not acquired this 'habit' by long use?...Nearly all natural instincts in animals have thus been formed as artificial reflexes in man. In man artificial habits formed at will replace instincts of fixed character, or, if you please, voluntary habits replace automatic habits. It is wonderful to note that even fixed habits that have passed long since into instincts or reflexes, can be modified by environment.... The force of habit is, however, very great, and is only short of natural reflexes, which are omnipotent in the body. No power of mind or will can stop the beating of the heart or the movement of the stomach, and a habit may be formed as to be almost as difficult to check. Darwin found that he had acquired, in common with most men, the habit of starting back at the sudden approach of danger; and no amount of will-power could enable him to keep his face pressed against the plate-glass front of the cage of the cobra in the Zoo while it struck at him, even though he exerted the full force of his will, and his reason told him there was no danger."

James says: "Whilst we are learning to walk, to ride, to swim, skate, fence, write, play or sing, we interrupt ourselves at every step by unnecessary movements and false notes. When we are proficient, on the contrary, the results follow not only with the very minimum of muscular action requisite to bring them forth, but they follow from a single instantaneous 'cue.' The marksman sees the bird, and, before he knows it, he has aimed and shot. A gleam in his adversary's eye, a momentary pressure from his rapier, and the fencer finds that he has instantly made the right parry and return. A glance at the musical hieroglyphics, and the pianist's fingers have rippled through a shower of notes. And not only is it the right thing at the right time that we thus involuntarily do, but the wrong thing also, if it be an habitual thing. Who is there that has never wound up his watch on taking off his waistcoat in the daytime, or taken his latch-key out on arriving at the door-step of a friend! Persons in going to their bedroom to dress for dinner have been known to take off one garment after another and finally to get into bed, merely because that was the habitual issue of the first few movements when performed at a later hour. We all have a definite routine manner of performing certain daily offices connected with the toilet, with the opening and shutting of familiar cupboards, and the like. But our higher thought-centres know hardly anything about the matter. Few men can tell off-hand which sock, shoe or trousers-leg they put on first. They must first mentally rehearse the act; and even that is often insufficient— the act must be *performed*. So of the questions, which valve of the shutters opens first? Which way does my door swing? etc. I cannot *tell* the answer; yet my *hand* never makes a mistake. No one can *describe* the order in which he brushes his hair or teeth; yet it is likely that the order is a pretty fixed one in all of us."

"Habit a second nature!" said the Duke of Wellington. "Habit is ten times nature!" Schneider says: "In the act of walking even when our attention is entirely absorbed elsewhere, it is doubtful whether we could preserve equilibrium if no sensation of our body's attitude were there, and doubtful whether we should advance our leg if we had no sensation of its movement as executed, and not even a minimal feeling of impulse to set it down. Knitting appears to be altogether mechanical, and the knitter keeps up her knitting even while she reads or is engaged in lively talk. But if we ask her how this is possible, she will hardly reply that the knitting goes on of itself. She will rather say that she has a feeling of it, and that she feels in her hands that she knits and how she must knit, and that therefore the movements of knitting are called forth and regulated by the sensations associated therewithal, even when the attention is called away." Huxley says: "There is a story which is credible enough, though it may not be true, of a practical joker who, seeing a discharged veteran carrying home his dinner, suddenly called out, 'Attention!' whereupon the man instantly brought his hands down, and lost his mutton and potatoes in the gutter."

Kay says: "In our first attempts to walk, to write, to play on an instrument, or to carry on any other operation, we are intensely conscious of every movement that we make. By degrees, as we acquire more ease and dexterity in their performance, we become less and less conscious of them, till we may come to perform them quite unconsciously." Stewart says: "An expert accountant can sum up almost with a single glance of his eye a long column of figures. He can tell the sum with unerring certainty, while at the same time he is unable to recollect any one of the figures of which that sum is composed, and yet nobody doubts that each of these figures has passed through his mind, or supposes that when the rapidity of the process becomes so great that he is unable to recollect the various steps of it, he obtains the result by a sort of inspiration."

Maudsley says: "When a beginner is learning his notes on the pianoforte, he has deliberately to call to mind each note; but, when, by frequent practice, he has acquired complete skill in playing on that instrument there is no conscious memory, but his movements are automatic." Kay says: "There are some who hold that when actions thus come to be performed unconsciously, the mind ceases to have any part in the direction of them." But this idea has been superseded by the theories of the subconscious mind which have arisen from a better acquaintance with the subject. As Stewart says: "In the case of some operations which are very familiar to us, we find ourselves unable to attend to or to recollect the acts of the will by which they were preceded; and accordingly some philosophers of great eminence have called in question the existence of such volitions, and have represented our habitual actions as involuntary and mechanical. But surely the circumstance of our inability to recollect our volitions does not authorize us to dispute their possibility, any more than our inability to attend to the process of the mind, in estimating the distance of an object from the eye, authorizes us to affirm that the perception is instantaneous."

Kay says: "The more we cultivate and train any power or faculty, the more easily and rapidly does it perform its work,— the less is consciousness concerned in it, the more work does it accomplish, and the less does it suffer from fatigue. Our mental progress, then, is in the direction of our becoming unconscious, or largely unconscious, of many of our activities. Consciousness has at first an important place in the training of our faculties and the building up of our knowledge. The more consciousness is concentrated upon any new operation, the more readily is it mastered; and the more it is concentrated upon any idea brought before the mind, the better is it impressed upon the memory. But as we acquire facility and skill in the operation, as the memory acquired strength we become less conscious of them." Maudsley says: "The interference of consciousness is often an actual hindrance to the association of ideas, as it notably is to the performance of movements that have attained the complete ease of an automatic execution." Morrell says: "In proportion as volition has to be exercised in carrying them on, in that proportion are they imperfectly performed, and then only at the expense of much labor and fatigue." Maudsley again says: "Consciousness does essential service in the building up of faculties of thought and action; its part is comparatively small in the use we make of them afterwards.... There is not a faculty of the mind which, though they began by using it consciously, they do not after habitual practice exercise unconsciously." Therefore, in view of the above, we may see the truth of Kay's statement: "The great object of education should be to transfer as much as possible of our actions from the conscious to the unconscious region of our mind. Schofield says: "Once a habit is well established on such lines as these, the interference of conscious will only spoils its perfect action. Whenever knitting or typewriting has become automatic, if you think about the formation of every stitch or letter, you have to work much more slowly, and are more liable to make mistakes. A fixed habit is thus deranged by volition. The more fixed a habit becomes, the less of the body is required to execute it, and thus a great economy of force is effected. In commencing piano playing, the young performer plays with her hands, and arms and body and head, and often her tongue. As she forms a perfect artificial relax, less and less of the body is moved, until at last it is literally nothing but the hands and wrists that are engaged, the conscious brain being at perfect rest, or thinking of something else altogether. Habit is thus of great economic value. Habit, which is physical memory, is of such importance to character that a brain without such memory is either idiotic or infantile. Artificial reflexes last long if well formed. Robert Houdin, the conjurer, trained himself in the difficult habit of reading aloud while keeping four balls going in the air. He did not practice this for many years, and yet after thirty years he found he could still read and keep three balls going. Anyone who tries this feat will understand its difficulty."

Schofield also says: "Ease and perfection in any pursuit entirely depend upon the degree in which it ceases to be connected with consciousness and is carried on subconsciously. Playing the piano, skating, bicycling, skilled trades, and indeed almost everything, depend for their perfect execution on the power of the subconscious mind, which is only hampered when interfered with by the conscious mind.... The marvels of playing a brilliant piece on the piano, while at the same time conducting a vigorous conversation, show also the greatness of our unconscious powers, especially when we remember that Sir James Paget has pointed out that in rapid playing the finger moves twenty-four times a second, each movement involving at least three muscular acts, which if multiplied by ten, gives 720 impulses *per second* for both hands." Miss Cobbe says: "The pen of a ready writer seems to dip itself into the ink at the right time, to form of itself all the words, and even to select different words to begin each sentence, and to avoid terminating them with prepositions, while all the time the conscious mind of the writer is deeply occupied with the plot."

The same authority says: "I would remark here that in what we call voluntary actions all we do is to will a *result*, as of raising the hand to the mouth. The ease with which we do it and indeed the power to do it at all arise, not from our will-power being able to control the so-called voluntary muscles, but in their association by unconscious mental action for the purpose by long established habit. Where no such habit exists an action becomes well-nigh impossible, however strongly it may be willed. By long habit, hereditary in nature, we always swing our right arm with the movement of our left leg, and the left arm with the right leg. Let anyone *will* to the contrary; that is to move the right arm with the right leg, and *vice versa*, and, however strong the effort of will may be, they will find in the end that it is powerless to overcome this established habit, except most awkwardly, and for the shortest time. The intense difficulty of the one movement and the perfect ease of the other, both in themselves equally easy, are most striking. Let anyone *will* to play the violin, or to skate, or to swim, or in short to do anything that requires the formation of habits, and they will see it is impossible and that to do so at all a habit must necessarily be formed for the very purpose; and then, behold! the thing which was impossible to perform by conscious will-power is executed by unconscious forces with almost contemptuous ease. Few of us know what bundles of habits we are, and we imagine many of our actions to be voluntary which are really artificially automatic. Let any man over forty try to wash and dress himself in any but the accustomed order, and he will see what difficulties arise. He may not know the order in which he washes his face—but the *hands* know. He cannot tell which foot is put into his stockings first—but the feet know. Before I begin to dress, from long habit I am almost compelled to pull up the blind a certain exact height, and if I fail to do so, I feel an inward impulse that is not satisfied till it is obeyed. Consider the habit of shooting—the perfect ease with which the trained sportsman, the moment the grouse rise, aims and fires well-nigh automatically at the birds, which themselves have acquired advanced habits (as Sir Joseph Fayrer has told us) in learning unconsciously to avoid the telegraph wires as they fly, which in earlier times they always struck against"

It has been said by eminent psychologists that over ninety percent of our mental processes are performed on the subconscious plane. A consideration of the facts above stated, in connection with mental habit, will show us that this statement is correct. As Prof. Gates has well said:

"At least ninety percent of our mental life is subconscious. If you will analyze your mental operations you will find that conscious thinking is never a continuous line of consciousness, but a series of conscious data with great intervals of subconsciousness. We sit and try to solve a problem and fail. We walk around, try again and fail. Suddenly an idea dawns that leads to a solution of the problem. The subconscious processes were at work. We do not volitionally create our own thinking. It takes place in us. We are more or less passive recipients. We cannot change the nature of a thought, or of a truth, but we can, as it were, guide the ship by a moving of the helm."

The woman who runs her sewing machine becomes so expert that she will proceed to execute the most intricate work thereon, and at the same time will be thinking of matters of an entirely different nature— perhaps may be glancing out of the window, but let something go wrong with the machine or the material—let the thread snap or something "get caught." and her subconscious mind will send a quick sharp command to its conscious companion and the attention will be on the work in a moment. The same thing is true of the typewriter who writes at a great rate of speed while thinking of her new hat, or how she will trim that dress that she is making over. In some cases she will *feel* that she has omitted a comma or couple of lines further back, and she will stop her writing to correct the error. Some schools of typewriting teach their pupils to write by touch—that is, without glancing at the keys, many of the pupils being able to write in the dark, or else blind-folded.

Likewise the compositor who sets up this book on the typesetting machine at a high rate of speed, does so more or less unconsciously. His fingers fly over the keys, and his eyes are fastened on the "copy," but although he feels the keys and sees the manuscript his mind is probably far away. He corrects our punctuation, and supplies a missing letter to some word— often finds it necessary to remedy errors in spelling (alas!) but while doing this he forms no conscious mental impression of the sense of what is being read, and when he leaves his work he is unable to tell whether it was a page of Pilgrim's Progress, one of Bernard Shaw's plays, or a chapter on Mental Habit! And, moreover, he will subconsciously read and set up the type of the above statement, and will be totally unconscious that we have been using him as an object lesson in our text. Moreover, the proofreaders who go over the work of the compositor will read the printed pages, detecting errors with a greater or less degree of skill, and will not be conscious of what it is all about— nor will they detect this reference to themselves, although one reads it to another. Unless the word "proof-reader" strikes their ear with a familiar sound, they will remain in blissful oblivion of the reference. But let someone at the other end of the room whisper something of a personal nature, and they will hear each word distinctly and will understand what is being said, even though the proof-reading proceeds without interruption.

Telegraph operators manifest the same degree and character of subconscious mentation. They will receive, or send, long messages without thinking of the subject, and remaining totally unconscious of the news that is being transmitted.

They pay no attention whatsoever, consciously, to the matter passing through their hands. It is related by the biographer of a noted electrician, that he was working in the main office of a telegraph company, in one of the large cities, when the news of the assassination of President Lincoln came over the wires in the shape of a press dispatch. The operator took down the news and wrote it on the sheet, and passed it on through the regular channels without realizing what the news was. It was simply a part of a long series of news-stuff that he was taking down. Later the details began coming in, but the operators did not consciously grasp the import of the messages although they took down every word of it. After several hours, one of the operators stopped work and went outside, where he saw by the newspaper extras that the President had been assassinated. He rushed back into the office and startled the operators with the news. They doubted it, and referred to their copies of the messages they had taken, when they saw that they had been receiving the news for several hours without realizing it. This is far from being an exceptional case, and is notable only by reason of the importance of the news in question.

Who does not travel over his accustomed route, to and from his work, without taking conscious notice of his steps and his progress. The same thing is noticeable to a greater degree when one has "something on his mind" and walks home preoccupied with his reveries or thoughts. Blocks are traversed, corners are turned, passing vehicles are avoided, automobiles are dodged—all unconsciously—and at the last the day-dreamer finds himself turning toward his own door-step, or flat entrance, and then only does he "wake up." It is the phenomena of the somnambulist, or sleepwalker, in a lesser degree. A consideration of the subject will convince any person that at least ninety percent of his mental activities are performed by his subconscious mind. The conscious mind is little more than the pilot at the wheel—the subconscious is the engineer down below in the mental engine-room.

In Suggestion and Auto-Suggestion, the New Psychology furnishes one with the secret of the Mastery of Habit. While it is true that Habit masters the individual, it is likewise true that the individual may create his own habits—may establish desirable habits, and neutralize and inhibit undesirable ones. Auto-Suggestion, properly used in a scientific manner, renders the individual the master in the end. In the volume of this series entitled Suggestion and Auto-Suggestion, we have given in detail the methods approved of and employed by eminent psychologists for the cultivation of desirable habits and the destruction of undesirable habits. The person who neglects this important subject places himself at a considerable disadvantage, and throws away one of the most effective mental weapons forged by modern science. In Auto-Suggestion we have the Key to Character Building, which includes the mastery of habit.

10

The Subconscious and the Body.

It is now generally conceded by the best authorities that the subconscious mind has charge and control of the activities and functions of the physical body. Many persons seem to think that the physical organs "run themselves" like the wheels of a watch which move in response to the wound-up spring. But there is ever in evidence the presence of mind in all of the activities of the body even to the movements and activities of the cells. Hudson's claim that "The subjective mind has absolute control of the functions, conditions and sensations of the body" has been corroborated by the later investigators. As Schofield says: "The unconscious mind, in addition to the three qualities which it shares in common with the conscious—*viz.*, will, intellect and emotion—has undoubtedly another very important one—nutrition, or the general maintenance of the body.

Von Hartmann says: "The explanation that unconscious psychical activity itself appropriately forms and maintains the body has not only nothing to be said against it, but has all possible analogies from the most different departments of physical and of animal life in its favor, and appears to be as scientifically certain as is possible in the inferences from effect to cause." Maudsley says: "The connection of mind and body is such that a given state of mind tends to echo itself at once in the body." Carpenter says: "If a psychosis or mental state is produced by a neurosis or material nerve state, as pain by a prick, so also is a neurosis produced by a psychosis. That mental antecedents call forth physical consequents is just as certain as that physical antecedents call forth mental consequents." Tuke says: "Mind, through sensory, motor, vaso-motor and trophic nerves, causes changes in sensation, muscular contraction, nutrition and secretion.... If the brain is an outgrowth from a body corpuscle and is in immediate relation with the structures and tissues that preceded it, then, though these continue to have their own action, the brain must be expected to act upon the muscular tissue, the organic functions and upon the nervous system itself." Tuke uses the word "brain" as synonymous with "mind."

Von Hartmann says: "In willing any conscious act, the unconscious will is evoked to institute means to bring about the effect. Thus, if I will a stronger salivary secretion, the conscious willing of this effect excites the unconscious will to institute the necessary means. Mothers are said to be able to provide through the will a more copious secretion, if the sight of the child arouses in them the will to suckle. There are people who perspire voluntarily. I now possess the power of instantaneously reducing the severest hiccoughs to silence by my own will, while it was formerly a source of great inconvenience to me.... An irritation to cough, which has no mechanical cause, may be permanently suppressed by the will. I believe we might possess a far greater voluntary power over our bodily functions if we were only accustomed from childhood to institute experiments and to practice ourselves therein...We have arrived at the conclusion that every action of the mind on the body, without exception, is only possible by means of an unconscious will; that such an unconscious will can be called forth partly by means of a conscious will, partly also through the conscious idea of the effect, without conscious will, and even in opposition to the conscious will."

Wundt says: "Mental phenomena cannot be referred to bodily as effects to causes, but there is a uniform coordination between mental processes and definite physical processes in the brain. The connection can only be regarded as a parallelism of two causal series side by side, but never directly interfering with each other, in virtue of the incompatibility of their terms. It is a psychophysical parallelism." Porter says: "All those inferences that unextended spirit and extended matter can have no relations with each other are set aside by the obvious facts that one *does* affect the other. The spirit can take the body, and by conscious and unconscious activities, mould it for a dwelling place and instrument for its uses, before it enters into possession by sensibility and intelligence."

Schofield says: "The mental centres in the cortex have the power of directly influencing physiological functions and tissue nutrition.... Going to sleep is undoubtedly largely the result of suggestions from the unconscious mind, which also brings a general feeling into consciousness when, on waking enough sleep has been had; or on the other hand, when it has been insufficient." Maudsley says: "The general bodily feeling which results from the sense of the different organic processes is not attended with any definite consciousness." Schofield adds: "But certain mental feelings seem connected with definite parts of the body—love with the heart and melancholy with the liver, while to arrive at the highest point of mental insight, there has always been a tendency to direct the thoughts to the pit of the stomach, or just above the navel; here lies the great solar plexus, chief center of the sympathetic system. Many feelings are connected with this region, and we speak of a sickening story, sickening thoughts, etc.... The organic or vegetative functions as well as the skin and hair are specially affected by the emotions. A short time of extreme trouble may make a man look many years older than before it commenced. The eye will lose its brightness, the face will become withered, the brow wrinkled and the hair blanched. Fear may check perspiration and produce skin diseases."

Carter quotes a case where: "A lady saw a heavy dish fall from her child's hand, cutting off three of the fingers. She felt great pain in her hand, and on examination the corresponding three were swollen and inflamed. In twenty-four hours incisions were made, and pus evacuated." Von Hartman says: "The influence of the most dissimilar emotions on the functions of secretion are well known; e. g., vexation and anger on bile and milk." James says: "The unconscious mind as revealed by hypnotism can exercise marvelous control over the nervous, vaso-motor and circulatory and other systems. A hypnotized person can hold out his arm indefinitely in painless contraction, can inhale strong ammonia under the name of attar of roses with unwatery eyes.... There seems to be no reasonable grounds for doubting that, in certain chosen subjects, congestion, burns, blisters, raised papules, bleeding from the nose or skin can be produced by suggestion." Braid says: "The expectation of a belief of something about to happen is quite sufficient to change the physical action of any part.... The sensation of heat and cold can be abolished by the unconscious mind, and high temperature produced in the blood by the same agency without disease."

Schofield says: "The effects of a purgative pill have been rendered *nil* and it has produced sleep in the belief it was an opiate pill, though consisting of a strong dose of colocynth and calomel. On the other hand, an opium pill given for sleep has failed to produce it, but proved a strong purgative in the belief it was so intended. Laughter stamps a merry look upon the face, which, by degrees, becomes permanent, and tends to produce a happy disposition. If you set your face truly to express a passion, you tend to feel that passion.... It is very curious how we place our body in attitudes corresponding to our mental states, just as we have already seen bodily attitudes may cause mental states. If we try to see a thing with our mind we often put on an intense and strained expression with our eyes. If we are in a state of delight the eyes are fixed in ecstasy. Some words almost seem to have a pleasant or disagreeable taste. How great grief paralyzes the body generally! Falling in love, too, affects the whole body, while the shock of breaking off an engagement may produce profound anemia, or blanch the hair in twenty-four hours."

Braid, who gave to hypnotism its name, says: "I passed a gold pencil-case from the wrist to the fingers of a lady fifty-six years old without touching her, and she experienced a creeping, twitching sensation in that hand until it become quite unpleasant. On getting her to look in another direction and describe her feelings, the results were the same when I made no movement at all, the whole being evidently caused by the power of the mind in causing a physical action of the body. With another lady I took a pair of scissors and passed them over her hand laid upon the table from the wrist downward without contact. She immediately felt a creeping sensation followed by spasmodic twitching of the muscles so as to toss the hand from the table. I then desired her to place her other hand on the table, so that she might not observe what was being done, and in the same length of time similar phenomena were manifested, though I did nothing. I then told her her hand would become cold, and it was so; then intensely hot.... A London physician, who mesmerized by the use of a powerful magnet, had a patient in a magnetic sleep. He told me the mere touch of a magnet would at once stiffen her which at once proved to be the case. I now told him I had a small instrument in my pocket which was quite as powerful, and offered to operate on his patient, whom I had never seen before, and who was asleep when I entered the room. My instrument was only three inches long, as thick as a quill, with a ring at the end. I told him, when put into her hands, both arms would become rigid, and such was the case. I then took the instrument from her, and again returned it to another position, and told him now it would have the reverse effect, and she would not be able to hold it; and now, if her hand was forcibly closed on it, it would open of itself, and such was the case, to the great surprise of the doctor, who wanted to know what had been done to the instrument to invest it with this opposite power. This I declined to tell him till he had seen the following proofs of its remarkable powers. I told him that a touch with it on either leg would cause the leg to rise and become rigid, and such was the case. That a second touch would relax the rigidity, and cause it to fall, which proved to be a fact. She then awoke. I then applied the ring of my instrument to the third finger of her right hand, from which it was suspended, and told the doctor it would send her asleep; to this he replied,

'It never will.' I told him again I was sure of it. We were then silent and she speedily fell asleep. Having roused her again, I put the instrument on the second finger of her left hand, and told the doctor it would be found she could not go to sleep when it was placed there. He said she would, and steadily gazed at her to send her off. After some time he asked her if she did not feel sleepy, to which she replied, 'Not at all.' I then requested her to look at the point of the forefinger of her right hand, which I told the doctor would send her to sleep, and such was the case. I then roused her, and made her go to sleep again by looking at the nail of the thumb of the left hand. I then explained to the doctor that the wonderful instrument which I had used was the key and ring of my portmanteau."

The above cases cited by Braid are typical cases of masked suggestion, and tend to prove the contention of the suggestionists that the phenomena of hypnotism are caused by suggestion pure and simple, instead of by the outward passes, instruments, and other fanciful accessories of the mesmerist.

They are quoted here for the purpose of illustrating the effect of accepted suggestions upon the subconscious planes of mentation, and the resulting physical manifestations.

Tuke quotes a case of a woman who was afflicted with a severe attack of acute rheumatism upon hearing that her husband had met with a serious accident. He says: "Pleasurable emotion gives firmness and regularity to the action of the heart, promotes the circulation of the blood, increases the gastric secretions, and imparts firmness and regularity to the muscular contractions of the stomach.... John Hunter says he was subject to spasm of his vital parts when anxious about any event; as, for instance, whether bees would swarm or not; whether the large cat he was anxious to kill would get away before he could get the gun." Dr. Leith said that he was "inclined to doubt whether the benefits of Nauheim (a treatment for the heart) were not after all to be explained largely, if not entirely, by the influence of the mental factor!" Malebranche relates that when he read Descartes' treatise *De l'homme* it caused such a violent beating of the heart by its wonderful power that he was obliged to lay it aside to breathe freely again.

Schofield says: "Joy increases the palpitation of the heart by increased vital action, terror does the same in another way. As a general principle, pleasurable emotions increase the vital functions, and painful ones depress them. The action of the heart is greatly affected by emotions through the sympathetic system; it is quickened or slowed or even stopped by mental shock through the tenth nerve. The movements of the heart are altered, and peculiarities of the beat are exaggerated when attention is closely fixed upon it.... During the rush of consumptives to Berlin for inoculation by Dr. Koch's tuberculin, a special set of symptoms were observed to follow the injection and were taken as being diagnostic of the existence of tuberculosis; amongst others, a rise of temperature after so many hours. These phenomena were eagerly looked for by the patients, and occurred accurately in several who were injected with pure water. The formation of blisters full of serum from the application of plain stamp and other paper to various parts of the bodies of patients in the hypnotic state, is well attested and undoubtedly true."

A writer in the "Proceedings of the Psychical Research Society" says: "Dr. R. von Krafft-Ebing has produced a rise from 37 degrees C. to 38.5 degrees in a patient whose mind was fixed by suggestion, and Dr. Binet has lowered the temperature of the hand 10 degrees C. 'How can it be,' he asks, 'when one merely says to the subject, "your hand will become cold," and the vaso-motor system answers by constricting the artery?'" Tuke says. "A lady saw a child in immediate danger of having its ankle crushed by an iron gate. She was greatly agitated, but could not move, owing to intense pain coming on in her corresponding ankle. She walked home with difficulty, took off her stocking and found a circle around the ankle of a light red color, with a large red spot on the outer side. By the morning her whole foot was inflamed, and she had to remain in bed for some days.... A young woman witnessing the lancing of an abscess in the axilla immediately felt pain in that region, followed by inflammation. Dr. Marmise of Bordeaux tells us of a lady's maid who, when the surgeon put his lancet into her mistress's arm to bleed her, felt the prick in her own arm, and shortly after there appeared a bruise at the spot."

Prof. Barrett says: "It is not so well known, but it is nevertheless a fact, that utterly startling physiological changes can be produced in a hypnotized subject merely by conscious or unconscious mental suggestion. Thus a red scar or a painful burn, or even a figure of definite shape, such as a cross or an initial, can be caused to appear on the body of an entranced subject solely by suggesting the idea. By creating some local disturbance of the blood-vessels in the skin, the unconscious self has done what it would be impossible for the conscious self to perform. And so in the well-attested cases of stigmata, where a close resemblance to the wounds on the body of the crucified Savior appear on the body of the ecstatic. This is a case of unconscious self-suggestion, arising from the intent and adoring gaze of the ecstatic upon the bleeding figure on the crucifix. With the abeyance of the conscious self, the hidden powers emerge, whilst the trance and mimicry of the wounds are strictly parallel to the experimental cases previously referred to. May not some of the well-known eases of mimicry in animal life originate, like the stigmata, in a reflex action, as physiologists would say, below the level of consciousness, created by a predominant impression analogous to those producing the stigmata? That is to say, to reflex actions excited by an unconscious suggestion derived from the environment; in other words, the dynamic, externalizing power of thought, if the action of that which is unconscious may be called thought. We must, in fact, extend our idea of 'thought' to something much wider than intellectuation or ideation— these are special acts of thought, for the direction of functional activity of our sub-liminal life has also the attributes of thought though we may be unconscious of its thinking."

Schofield says: "The will can produce a cough, but not a sneeze. Hysterical (or mind) cough, and *dyspnoea* or short breath are well known. One cannot breathe naturally when the action is brought into full consciousness When a patient is told to breathe naturally, and tries hard to do so, the results are often ludicrous. Emotions produce a feeling of suffocation, and the rising of a ball in the throat. The breath is altered by the emotions. The short quiet breath of joy contrasts with the long sigh of relief after breathless suspense. Joy gives *eupnaea* or easy breathing, grief or rather fear tends to *dyspnoea* or difficult breathing. Sobbing goes with grief, laughter with joy, and one often merges into the other. Yawning is produced by pure idea or by seeing it, as well as by fatigue. Dr. Morton Prince says a lady he knew always had violent catarrh in the nose (hay fever) if a rose was in the room. He gave her an artificial one and the usual symptoms followed. He then showed her it was a false one, and had no pollen, etc., and ever after all symptoms disappeared. How many cases of hay fever have a somewhat similar origin in the unconscious mind...Respiration is almost suspended in strong intellectual work. We both see and hear best when not breathing...The hair may be turned gray and white by emotion in a few hours or sooner...If the thoughts are strongly directed to the intestinal canal, as by bread pills, it will produce strong peristaltic action. Vomiting occurs from mental causes, apart from organic brain disease. Bad news will produce nausea; emotion also, or seeing another person vomit, or certain smells or ideas, or thoughts about a sea-voyage, or the thought that an emetic has been taken. The thought of food produces a copious flow of gastric juices in the stomach and saliva in the mouth. Hysterical dyspepsia, eructation, vomiting and gastralgia are all common.... The thought of an acid fruit will fill the mouth with water. A successful way of stopping discordant, street-music is to suck a lemon within full view of a German band. Fear will so dry the throat that dry rice cannot be swallowed. This is a test in India for the detection of a murder. The suspected man is brought forward and given a handful of rice to swallow. If he can do this he is innocent; if he cannot he is guilty, fear having dried up his mouth. Vomiting in cases of poisoning is not always from stomach irritation. In some cases it is the result of a protective mechanism. Similarly we get loss of appetite in bilious attacks. Dr. Murchison says there is good evidence that nerve influence may not only cause functional derangement, but also cure structural disease of the liver. A young lady who could not be cured of vomiting was engaged to be married. On being told that the wedding day must be postponed till cured, the vomiting ceased. Sir James Paget tells us of very severe *parotitis* or inflammation of the salivary gland occurring in a man of sixty-nine from the sight of acid food. When a boy he was always upset at the sight of vinegar."

And now having listened to the testimony regarding the effect of the subconscious mind on the body, let us proceed to a consideration of the effect of suggestion, through the subconscious mind, over diseased conditions of the body. This phase of the subject gives us the most convincing evidence of the existence of the subconscious mind, and its dominant power over the physical functions.

From the most ancient times there have been various forms and methods of influencing the subconscious mind in the direction of causing it to exert itself to bring about normal functioning of the physical organs and parts of the body. Under various guises—by the use of various symbols—by the employment of various methods—under various names—has this form of therapy been practiced. In the majority of cases it has been masked under the form of religion or semi-religious ceremonies of higher or lower degree. And, likewise, it is often found masquerading under the guise or symbol of some fanciful contrivance, remedy, or appliance supposed to possess therapeutic value. But, under all of these guises and cloaks, the psychologist is able to discern the form of the familiar use of suggestion for the purpose of inciting the subconscious mind to activity and normal functioning.

Among the tribes of Africa we find the caste of magicians or medicine-men, who with quaint and grotesque ceremonies charm the disease away from the tribesmen. Many of these magicians are impostors, while many are neurotic individuals who work themselves up to a state of emotional frenzy which is accepted as a sure mark of superhuman power. In Australia we find the *koonkie* who claims to have the power of transferring the disease from the body of the afflicted person to a bit of leaf, wood or earth. In Hawaii we find the *kahuna*, who pow-wows over the sick person and charms away his ailment. In Siberia we find the *shaman*, or healing-priests, who claim to have divine power to cure diseases, and who often throw themselves into trances in their desire to show a visible sign of their great power. In the Antilles we find the *bohuti* who heals by means of ecstatic gyrations and manifest trickery. In China we find the fox-priest who claims to possess the power to drive away the demonic foxes who are gnawing at the vitals of the sufferer. In Japan there are several castes of priests who have a monopoly in certain sections in the matter of charming away disease by mystical and religious ceremonies. In India the religious healers' name is legion. On all sides they swarm with their prayers, charms and incantations.

Not only in modern times, but in the most ancient as well, the priestly medicine man was in evidence. In Assyria and Babylon the priests had developed the art of driving away the tormenting demons by their magical arts. Among the Jews the priests cured by prayer and ceremonies. The Egyptians had their sacred temples in which the sick were restored to health, and the priests with the gift of healing. The Greeks and Romans had their shrines and holy places where the diseased might become whole once more, after bestowing alms and fees upon the priests. In short wherever men have lived there have been found these religious or semi-religious methods of healing disease. And even to-day, we find the practice in full vigor, with its various forms of sacred shrines, saintly relics, religious formulae, and various "movements" in which religion and psychotherapy are co-mingled, often grotesquely.

The modern psychologist brushes away with a bold hand the mystery underlying these priestly cures. He sees in evidence always the principle of suggestion in operation in the direction of stimulating the subconscious mind toward correct physical functioning. The principle underlying these cures is very simple in its basic elements and in its methods. An understanding of the methods will enable anyone to duplicate the most wonderful of the religious cures, providing the conditions are equally favorable. It is very true that the religious emotion stimulates into intense activity the powers of the subconscious mind, and often to a degree not to be equaled by any other form of appeal. But science now understands that the object of the faith, or the particular form of the religion has absolutely nothing to do with the cure, the entire therapeutic value being inherent in the mental condition of the patient.

But it is not only in the field of religio-therapy that we must confine our investigation of this subject of subconscious cures. We find history filled with references to the principle in some of its various forms of manifestation. For instance, the cure of scurvy at the siege of Breda, in 1625. The entire garrison was suffering from scurvy, and the condition was critical. The Prince of Orange managed to secure three small vials of camphor, and after great rejoicing and appropriate ceremonies, including the public mixing of the unknown drug into many gallons of water a few drops of the mixture was administered to each man, the result being that the men rapidly recovered and the town was saved. Sir Humphrey Davy had a case of a patient suffering from a serious complaint. Wishing to test his temperature he inserted the clinical thermometer in the patient's mouth, under his tongue. The man imagined that it was some new and wonderful device for restoring him to health, and declared himself as much better at once. Continued treatment along the same lines effected a perfect cure in a few days. Dr. Gerbe of Pisa, cured several hundred cases of toothache among the citizens by causing the sufferers to crush a small insect between their fingers, after being gravely and solemnly informed that this was an infallible specific.

Schofield relates the following interesting cases: "A surgeon took into a hospital ward some time ago, a little boy who had kept his bed for five years, having hurt his spine in a fall. He had been all the time paralyzed in his legs, and could not feel when they were touched or pinched; nor could he move them in the least degree. After careful examination, the surgeon explained minutely to the boy the awful nature of the electric battery, and told him to prepare for its application next day. At the same time he showed him a sixpence, and sympathizing with his state, told him that the sixpence should be his if, notwithstanding, he should have improved enough the next day to walk leaning on and pushing a chair, which would also save the need of the battery. In two weeks the boy was running races in the park, and his cure was reported in the *Lancet*...A young lady who had taken ether two and a half years before, on the inhaler being held three inches away from the face, and retaining a faint odor of ether, went right off, and became unconscious without any ether being used or the inhaler touching her face...A woman was brought on a couch into a London hospital by two ladies who said that she had been suffering from incurable paralysis of the spine for two years, and having exhausted all their means in nursing her, they now sought to get her admitted, pending her removal to a home for incurables. In two hours I had cured her by agencies which owed all their virtue to their influence on the mind, and I walked with the woman half-a-mile up and down the waiting room, and she then returned home in an omnibus, being completely cured. An amusing case is that of a paralyzed girl, who, on learning that she had secured the affections of the curate, who used to visit her, got out of bed and walked,—cured; and afterward made an excellent pastor's wife. A remarkable instance of this sort is that of a child afflicted with paralysis, who was brought up from the country to Paris to the Hotel Dieu. The child who had heard a great deal of the wonderful metropolis, its magnificent hospitals, its omnipotent doctors, and their wonderful cures, was awe-struck, and so vividly impressed with the idea that such surroundings must have a curative influence, that the day after her arrival she sat up in bed much better. The good doctor just passed round, but had no time to treat her till the third day; by which time when he came round she was out of bed walking about the room, quite restored by the glimpses she had got of his majestic presence."

The interesting case of Elijah Perkins gives us a very good idea of what may be accomplished by arousing the expectant attention and faith of the public in some new contrivance or method which is absolutely devoid of therapeutic qualities in itself. We quote from Dr. Patton who says: "The most consummate proof of the verity of our text is furnished by a delusion that had its origin in our own country a century ago. An ignorant blacksmith, Elijah Perkins of Connecticut, during spare moments at his forge, welded together various metals, in an endeavor to fabricate a composition which would cure disease when applied to the surface of the body. Eventually he declared that he had succeeded, and he exhibited what he styled his 'Metallic Tractors,' really a pair of tongs about six inches long, one prong of brass, the other of steel. They were applied over, or as near the diseased parts as possible, always in a downward direction, for about ten minutes. The tractors were tried in every variety of internal and external ailments, with curative results so extraordinarily wonderful that they seemed to be effected by the direct agency of Almighty power, and not by natural agency. The treatment was called 'Perkinism,' in honor of the inventor. The demand for the tractors could not be supplied. The craze raged through the New England States, and spread to Great Britain and portions of Continental

Europe, where hospitals were established as fountains of health for suffering humanity. Within a brief period 1,500,000 cures were reported in Europe alone. While the delusion was at its height, Dr. Haygarth of London determined to ascertain how far the effects might be ascribed to the imagination. He accordingly formed pieces of wood into the shape of tractors, and with much assumed pomp and ceremony applied them to a number of sick persons who had been previously prepared to expect something extraordinary. The effects were found to be astonishing. Obstinate pains in the limbs were suddenly cured; joints that had long been immovable were restored to motion, and in short, except the renewal of lost parts or the change in mechanical structure, nothing seemed beyond their power to accomplish."

The science of Suggestive Therapeutics, which is so rapidly pushing itself forward to-day, and which is meeting with the approval and commendation of the best minds of the race, is based upon the recognition of the existence of the subconscious activities of the mind, and their effect upon the physical organism. Suggestive Therapeutics, or Psycho-Therapy, has for its basic working principle the fact the subconscious is amenable to suggestion, and that by means of suggestion the subconscious activities may be directed toward the restoring of normal functioning of the physical organs. In the volume of this series, entitled "Suggestion and Auto-Suggestion," we have devoted much space to the subject of Suggestive Therapeutics. We refer to this volume the reader who may desire to pursue the subject further.

11
Twilight Regions.

In the preceding chapters we have considered the phenomena of certain subconscious regions of the mind-regions which lie below the field of every-day consciousness. We have seen how these planes of mentation manifest activities resulting from past impressions, racial or individual, that have been placed there. The subconscious mind, proper, creates nothing but works manifold changes and variety among the stored up impressions of the past which have been deposited there. Toward the close of this book we speak of the *super*-conscious regions of the mind, in which are manifested activities new to the race, and which have not been experienced by the race or the individual. In this higher, or superconscious region, are contained the seed thoughts which will bear fruit in the future generations of the race, and which occasionally manifest in flashes of higher mentation in the minds of some of the race today. The subconscious is the result of the past—the superconscious belongs to the future.

But, other than these two great regions of the mind there are found regions which are difficult to classify. Using an imperfect illustration, we might say that the subconscious activities are like the lower notes on the keyboard of a piano, while the superconscious activities are like the upper notes. Then where are to be found these *other* activities which seem to be neither higher nor lower? Using the same illustration we may say that these *other* activities are like the *sharps and flats* on the keyboard—the black-keys. These *other* activities—these sharps and flats of the mental scale—are the manifestations of what are generally known as "psychic phenomena," by which term is meant the psychological phenomena which is more or less unusual, unclassified, unaccounted for, or possibly abnormal. It is true that many of the leading psychologists refuse to consider the said phenomena, and either classify it as "not proven" or else reject it altogether. But in view of the number of leading scientific authorities who testify to their experiences along these lines, and the work of the investigators of the Society for Psychical Research, we feel that we should at least give a brief consideration to the phenomena in question, in this work. For, if we admit the genuineness of the phenomena, or any part of it, we must include it in the category of the activities of the great Infra-Conscious regions of mentation. And the day has passed for blunt denial The phenomena exists, although not explained at present, and there is no reason whatsoever for relegating it to the field of the "supernatural," for it clearly belongs to the realm of the natural activities of the mind. So let us briefly consider this phase of the subject, at least in so far as the phenomena seems to be concerned with mental activities. We shall not attempt to enter into the field of the phenomena of what has been called "spiritualism," for that would take us out of the legitimate field of the present work.

Hudson attributed to his "subjective mind" the quality of telepathy, clairvoyance, second-sight, etc.,—considering them to be forms of telepathy as manifested by the subjective mind. He also attributed to it the quality of *telekinesis* or the moving of ponderable bodies. He said: "There are several ways by which the operations of the subjective mind can be brought above the threshold of consciousness. When this is done by any one of the various methods, phenomena are produced. Each of these phenomena has been, at some time in the history of mankind, attributed to the agency of disembodied spirits. The leading phenomena above alluded to are clairvoyance, clairaudience, telepathy, mesmerism, or hypnotism, automatic writing, percussive sounds {spirit-rapping), movements of ponderable bodies {table-tipping), and phantasmic appearances. Of these clairvoyance, telepathy, and hypnotism have generally ceased to be regarded as proceeding from supernatural agencies. They are now recognized as powers inherent in mankind, and, as will be seen, are largely employed to explain other phenomena."

Let us run rapidly over the various forms of psychic phenomena which are concerned with the Infra-Conscious regions of the mind.

Hypnotism is undoubtedly a phenomenon of the subconscious mind. While suggestions may be, and frequently are, accepted by the conscious mind, what are known as "hypnotic suggestions" are accepted only by the subconscious mind when the conscious faculties have been lulled into a passive or sleep condition. When this state is produced, the subconscious mind accepts the suggestions of an outside person and will proceed to reason from premises supplied it, as pointed out by Hudson from whom we have quoted on this point in a previous chapter. In such condition suggestions have an exaggerated effect, and impressions may be made upon the subconscious mind which tend to persist alter the person is aroused from the hypnotic state. There are many things about hypnotism which should prevent persons from indulging in its practices, and we would caution our readers against allowing themselves to be placed in this condition.

Telepathy, or Thought Transference, belong to the subconscious plane of the mind. Without attempting to consider any of the various theories advanced by the different schools, it must be held that whatever the theory regarding the *transmission* of the mental messages it is certain that the *receiving* of the message must be a function of the subconscious mind, or at least a faculty of the Infra-Conscious mentality. It certainly lies outside of the realm of the conscious faculties.

Clairvoyance, or Distant Sight, must also belong to the realm of the Infra-Conscious, no matter what hypothesis or theory concerning it we may entertain. Many authorities hold it to be but a form of Telepathy, while others hold that it is a phenomenon *sui generis*, that is, apart and distinct from telepathy or other psychic phenomena.

Psychometry, and similar phenomena, including Crystal Gazing and other forms of Distant Sensing, while far from explainable on any accepted psychological theory, nevertheless, if accepted at all, must be considered as belonging to the Infra-Conscious field or mental activities.

It is most difficult to classify phenomena of this sort, for while they do not belong to the superconscious activities, still they can scarcely be considered as an inherited experience of the subconscious. It is true that among some of the lowliest races of mankind there are to be found individuals possessing these powers, just as we find individuals among the most cultured manifesting them. It does not seem to be a matter of "high" or "low" but rather something running parallel to and along with our ordinary planes of consciousness—something in the nature of "sharps and flats" as we have said.

We shall not attempt to enter into any theoretical discussion regarding these *other* activities of the Infra-Conscious mentality. Our concern in this work is entirely with the more common and normal activities of the regions in question. To attempt to consider these *other* activities would result in extending this work far beyond its reasonable limits in space as well as in subject. We have noticed the existence of the phenomena in question, in passing, principally for the reason that, otherwise, it might be assumed that we ignored or denied them. Such phenomena belong rather to the field of Psychic Research than to

Psychology, at least in the state of the present knowledge of the subject. There have been many books written during the past decade, dealing with the subject of Psychical Research, to which we must refer the reader who wishes to pursue this phase of the subject further.

Before leaving this phase of the subject, however, we feel that we should mention an idea of our own, for what it is worth, which we have incorporated in another volume of this series.

Quoting from the said volume, we repeat at this place:

We allude to the possession of certain lower forms of unusual psychic power by some persons, which forms lack the elements of the so-called higher powers just alluded to, but which are still outside of the ordinary forms of sense-impressions—by some these phases of phenomena are called the "lower psychic faculties." The persons possessing and manifesting these powers are often far from being advanced spiritually, mentally, or morally, and this fact has surprised and perplexed many of the investigators of the subject. This class of phenomena differs materially from that of the superconsciousness, and evidently belongs to a lower plane—and yet, to *what* plane? Not to consciousness, surely, and if the subconsciousness is merely a record of race impressions and individual experiences, etc., how can these phenomena be credited to it? We have thought it likely that these "lower psychic" activities may be the survival of faculties formerly exercised by the race, but since discarded in the course of evolution, and now found only as vestigial remnants in some of the race. This view finds corroboration in a study of the mental activities of the lower animals, and primitive races of man, in both of which we find evidences of "sensing" other than those manifested by man. The animals and lower races have a sense of smell almost abnormal to civilized man, and they may have, and seem to have, other means of "sensing" objects. If this be true, then each of us must have some record of these discarded senses in our subconsciousness, which in some cases give rise to those instances of strange "awareness" noted in certain people, and which belong to the class of the "lower psychic" phenomena, as distinguished from the "higher psychic" phenomena belonging to the class of genius, intuition, spirituality, etc. We do not insist upon this theory—it is merely a conjecture, offered for what it is worth. It certainly seems to "fill in" a gap in the study of abnormal psychology.

12

The Superconscious.

We have seen that in the Infra-Conscious region of the mind there are certain activities which seem to be outside of the category of those which belong strictly to the subconscious—activities which cannot be considered as resulting from the past race or individual experience along the lines of racial memory or heredity, or of the memory of the individual—and yet which do not fit into the category of the "parallel" activities which we have classified as "the psychic." In short these activities seem rather to belong to a higher rather than a lower or even parallel plane of consciousness.

The Orientals for centuries have recognized these activities and have classified them as belonging to the "superconscious" plane of mentation—a plane above the ordinary plane of consciousness, just as the subconscious is a plane below it, and the "psychic" plane parallel to it. The superconscious plane is a plane of "above-consciousness," just as the subconscious is a plane "below-consciousness."

That the mind of man contains possibilities of activities as yet not generally unfolded into actual manifestation has been recognized by many writers on the subject, for many years. Isaac Taylor has told us that: "Perhaps within the field occupied by the visible and ponderable universe there is existing and moving another element fraught with other species of life— corporeal, indeed, and various in its orders, but not open to the cognizance of those who are confined to the conditions of animal organization...Is it to be thought that the eye of man is the measure of the Creator's power?—and has he created nothing which he has not exposed to our senses? The contrary seems much more than barely possible; ought we not to think it almost certain!" Masson says: "If a new sense or two were added to the present normal number in man, that which is now the phenomenal world for all of us might, for all we know, burst into something amazingly wider and different, in consequence of the additional revelations through these new senses."

Barret has said: "The mysteriousness of our being is not confined to subtle psychological processes which we have in common with all animal life. There are higher and more capacious powers wrapped up in our human personality than are expressed even by what we know of consciousness, will or reason. There are supernormal and transcendental powers of which at present we only catch occasional glimpses; and behind and beyond the supernormal there are fathomless abysses, the divine ground of the soul; the ultimate reality of which our consciousness is but the reflection or faint perception. Into such lofty themes I do not propose to enter, they must be forever beyond the scope of human inquiry; nor is it possible within the limits of this paper to give any adequate conceptions of those mysterious regions of our complex personality, which are open to, and beginning to be disclosed by, scientific investigation." Dr. Murray says: "Deeper down than where the soul with its consciousness can enter, there is spirit matter linking man with God; and deeper down than the mind and feelings or will—in the unseen depths of the hidden life—there dwells the Spirit of God."

Schofield says: "...so we may say that the mind includes not only the visible or conscious part, and what we have termed the subconscious...but the supraconscious mind that lies at the other end—all those regions of higher soul and spirit life, of which we are only at times vaguely conscious, but which always exist, and link us on to eternal verities.... The mind, indeed, reaches all the way, and while on the one hand it is inspired by the Almighty, on the other hand it energizes the body, all of whose purpositive life it originates. We may call the supraconscious mind the sphere of the spirit life, the subconscious the sphere of the body life, and the conscious mind the middle region where both meet.... The Spirit of God is said to dwell in believers, and yet, as we have seen, His presence is not the subject of direct consciousness. We would include, therefore, in the supraconscious, all such spiritual ideas, together with conscience—the voice of God, as Max Muller calls it— which is surely a half conscious faculty. Moreover, the supraconscious, like the subconscious, is, as we have said, best apprehended when the conscious mind is not active. Visions, meditations, prayers, and even dreams have been undoubtedly occasions of spiritual revelations, and many instances may be adduced as illustrations of the workings of the Spirit apart from the action of reason or mind. The truth apparently is that the mind as a whole is an unconscious state, by that its middle registers, excluding the highest spiritual and lowest spiritual manifestations, are fitfully illuminated in varying degrees by consciousness; and that it is this illuminated part of the dial that the word 'mind' which rightly appertains to the whole, has been limited." The above authority then quotes approvingly, the thought of another writer who says: "There are operations in us which transcend the limitations of ordinary faculties of cognition and which yet remain, not below the threshold, but rather above the horizon of our consciousness."

Ladd who is quite conservative, says: "A thinker on any problem finds the truth shot up from the hidden depths below; it appears presented for seizure to consciousness as the gift of the Unconscious. In similar fashion are the happy hits of the inventors, the rare achievements of art...*bestowed upon* the mind rather than consciously wrought out by it. Nor can one fail to notice as significant the connection of all such experiences with the condition and nature of 'tact,' of 'instinct.' If, then, credit is to be given, as it were, to the unconscious activities of our own mind for these results in consciousness which follow states of unconsciousness, such credit must be extended quite indefinitely. For the credit of much of our most brilliant and impressive acts in consciousness undoubtedly belongs not to consciousness; it belongs to somewhat or some One of whose doings we, as conscious egos, are not immediately conscious."

Von Hartmann says: "The Unconscious often guides men in their actions by hints and feelings when they could not help themselves by conscious thought. The Unconscious furthers the conscious process of thought by its inspirations in small as well as in great matters, and in mysticism guides mankind to the presentment of higher supersensible unities. The Unconscious makes men happy through the feeling for the beautiful and the artistic. If we institute a comparison between the conscious and the Unconscious, it is obvious there is a sphere which is always reserved to the Unconscious, because it remains forever inaccessible to the conscious." The same writer says: "That the Unconscious can readily outdo all the performances of conscious reason is seen in those fortunate natures that possess everything that others must acquire by toil, who never have a struggle with conscience, because they always spontaneously act correctly with feeling, and can never deport themselves otherwise than with tact, learn everything easily, complete everything they begin with a happy knack, live in eternal harmony with themselves, without ever reflecting much what they do, or ever experiencing difficulty and toil.

The fairest specimens of these instinctive natures are only seen in women. But what disadvantage lies in this self-surrender to the Unconscious? This—that one never knows where one is, or what one has; that one gropes in the dark, while one has got the lantern of consciousness in one's pocket; that it is left to accident whether the inspiration of the unconscious will come when one wants it; that one has no criterion but success. The conscious is an ever-ready servant, whose obedience may be always compelled; the Unconscious protects us like a fairy, and has always something uncomfortably demoniac about it. I may be proud of the work of consciousness, as my own deed, the fruit of my own hard labor; the fruit of the Unconscious is, at it were, a gift of the gods; it can therefore only teach me humility. The Unconscious is complete from top to toe, and must therefore be taken just as it is."

It will be noticed that in the phenomena of the superconscious, there is always the impression and idea of the flashes of thought or feeling coming from *above*—either from some higher part of one's own mind; the mind of some higher being; or the Universal Kind. There is always this impression or sense of the thought coming from *above*, although we may differ materially in our theories of ideas of what this "above" may be. From this above comes the inspiration of the artist, writer, poet or sculptor— the inventor has testified that some of his ideas have come to him like flashes from the blue. Speakers, preachers, orators, actors and many others have testified to their experiences in the direction of receiving ideas from *above*. Inspiration and intuition are always marked by this sense of the conscious mind, or field of consciousness, being *below* the source of the inspiration or intuition, never *above* it. So impressed is this upon the human mind, that one involuntarily raises the eyes and uplifts the face when speaking of some experience of this kind. It is easy to see why man has naturally fallen into the habit of thinking of the spiritual regions, or regions of higher life, as being *above*—although there is no "above" or "below" in space. There is the idea—which is in itself intuitional—that these exalted phases of mentation belong to a *higher* plane of mind—something *above*, more elevated, exalted. Perhaps a little consideration may show us why this is so.

In our first volume of the present series, we said regarding the Superconscious: "In the first place, instead of being the greater memory, or storehouse of the impressions of the past, as is the subconscious, the superconsciousness of the individual is *the latent possibilities* of the future man, or superman. And the flashes from this region that occasionally reach the field of consciousness are practically *the prophecies of the future of the race.* That which is now the superconscious region of the individual will someday become the ordinary plane of everyday mentation of the advanced race. The superconsciousness is the consciousness of the future individuals of the race, and in it are stored the latent faculties and mental activities of a higher race of beings. To some favored ones of the present race there come flashes from this wonderful region of the mind, and we call this 'genius,' 'intuition,' and other terms denoting higher and uncommon mental activities and states. In each individual there is stored this great reservoir of future mental development—why, or how, we do not know— but that it *is* we do know. Just as the oak tree dwells latent within the acorn; just as the coming Shakespeare, Milton, Darwin or Spencer was at one time latent within a single cell, so are these latent faculties and powers in the mind of each and every individual, awaiting the stroke of the clock of evolutionary unfoldment. And when these flashes pass down into the field of consciousness, we recognize them as coming from *above*, and not from *below*. The mental evolution of the race is not alone a matter of growth in the sense of addition—it is in the nature of an *unfoldment* of the latent qualities, faculties, and powers inherent in the mind, or perhaps the unfoldment into expression of some inherent power or quality of the Ego. At any rate it is undoubtedly an unfoldment—a revealing of something that has been hidden away from sight and expression...The man of to-day is slowly, laboriously, but surely unfolding into greater and grander mental states and activities. Mental growth comes not alone from without—there is an inner urge constantly at work, pressing ever on toward higher and greater things."

But, it will be urged, there cannot be an *unfoldment* unless there has first been a *folding up*—there can be no *evolution* without a previous *involution*. Anything *evolved* must first have been *involved*. Something can never proceed from nothing— unless by "nothing" we mean something existing in latency. And so it must be in the case before us. To explain how the involving process occurs would take us out of the field of

75

psychology into that of metaphysics, and we must beware of trespassing in the latter field. But we are probably warranted in calling your attention to the bearing upon the subject before us of the philosophical conception of a Universal Mind, or World Soul, in which the individual minds or souls are but centres of activity, or units of expression. If this be granted then we may see how it is possible for the mind to unfold latent powers and qualities transcending the individual and race experience, for in this case the latency would abide in the Universal Mind and the latter would afford an unlimited source for transcendent power and qualities. Let us see what the philosophers, and others, have to say regarding this One Source of mental power—this Transcendent One Mind.

The Oriental Philosophy is well expressed by Swami Vivekananda, in the following passage:

"Where is there any more misery for him who sees this Oneness in the Universe, this Oneness of life, Oneness of everything?

...This separation between men and man, man and woman, man and child, nation and nation, earth and moon, moon and sun, this separation between atom and atom is the cause of all the misery, and the Vedanta says this separation does not exist, it is not real. It is merely apparent on the surface. In the heart of things there is unity still. If you go inside you find that unity between man and man, women and children, races and races, high and low, rich and poor, the gods and men: all are One, and the animals too, if you go deep enough, and he who has attained to that has no more delusion. ...where is there any more delusion for him? What can delude him? He knows the reality of everything, the secret of everything. Where is there any more misery for him? What does he desire? He has traced the reality of everything unto the Lord, that centre, that Unity of everything, and that is Eternal Bliss, Eternal Knowledge, Eternal Existence. ...In the Centre, the reality, there is no one to be mourned for, no one to be sorry for. He has penetrated everything...When man has seen himself as One with the infinite Being of the universe, when all separateness has ceased, when all men, all women, all angels, all gods, all animals, all plants, the whole universe has been melted into that Oneness, then all fear disappears. Whom to fear? Can I hurt myself? Can I kill myself? Can I injure myself? Do you fear yourself? Then will all sorrow disappear. What can cause me sorrow? I

76

am the One Existence of the universe. Then all jealousies will disappear; of whom to be jealous. Of myself? Then all bad feelings disappear. Against whom shall I have this bad feeling? Against myself?

There is none in the universe but me. Kill out this differentiation, kill out this superstition that there are many. 'He who, in this world of many, sees that One, he who, in this mass of insentiency, sees that One Sentient Being; he who in this world of shadow, catches that Reality, unto him belongs eternal peace, unto none else, unto none else.'"

The Western Philosophy is beautifully expressed by Emerson in his wonderful essay, "The Oversoul," from which we shall quote here. Emerson says:

"The philosophy of six thousand years has not searched the chambers and magazines of the soul. In its experiments there has always remained in the last analysis, a residuum it could not resolve. Man is a stream whose source is hidden. Always our being is descending into us from we know not whence. The most exact calculator has no prescience that something incalculable may not baulk the very next moment. I am constrained every moment to acknowledge a higher origin for events than the will I call mine. As it is with events, so is it with thoughts. When I watch that flowing river, which out of regions I see not, pours for a season its streams into me,—I see that I am a pensioner,—not a cause but a surprised spectator of this ethereal water; that I desire and look up and put myself in the attitude of reception, but from some alien energy the visions come. The Supreme Critic on all the errors of the past and the present, and the only prophet of that which must be is that great nature in which we rest as the earth lies in the soft arms of the atmosphere; that Unity, that Over-Soul, within which every man's particular being is contained and made one with all other; that common heart of which all sincere conversation is the worship, to which all right action is submission; that overpowering reality which confutes our tricks and talents, and constrains every one to pass for what he is, and to speak from his character and not from his tongue, and which evermore tends to pass into our thought and hand and become wisdom and virtue and power and beauty. We live in succession, in division, in parts, in particles. Meantime within man is the soul of the whole; the wise silence; the universal beauty; to which every part and particle is equally related; the Eternal *One*.... We see the world piece by piece, as the sun, the moon, the animal, the tree; but the whole, of which these are the shining parts, is the soul....

"Words from a man who speaks from that life must sound vain to those who do not dwell in the same thought on their own part. I dare not speak for it. My words do not carry its august sense; they fall short and cold. Only itself can inspire whom it will, and behold! their speech shall be lyrical, and sweet, and universal as the rising of the wind. Yet I desire, even by profane words, if sacred I may not use, to indicate the heaven of this deity and to report what hints I have collected of the transcendent simplicity and energy of the Highest Law.

"All goes to show that the soul in man is not an organ; is not a function, like the power of memory, of calculation, of comparison,— but uses these as hands and feet; is not a faculty, but a light; is not the intellect or the will, but the master of the intellect and the will—is the vast background of our being, in which they lie,—an immensity not possessed and that cannot be possessed. From within or from behind, a light shines through us upon things, and makes us aware that we are nothing, but the light is all. What we commonly call man....does not, as we know him, represent himself, but misrepresents himself. Him we do not respect, but the soul, whose organ he is, would he let it appear through his action, would make our knees bend. When it breathes through his intellect, it is genius; when it breathes through his will, it is virtue; when it flows through his affection, it is love. And the blindness of the intellect begins when it would be something of itself. The weakness of the will begins when the individual would be something of himself. All reform aims in some one particular to let the great soul have its way through us; in other words, to engage us to obey.

"The sovereignty of this nature whereof we speak is made known by its independency of those limitations which circumscribe us on every hand. The soul circumscribeth all things. As I have said, it contradicts all experience. In like manner it abolishes time and space. The influence of the senses has in most men overpowered the mind to that degree that the wails of time and space have come to look solid, real and insurmountable; and to speak with levity of these limits is, in the world, the sign of insanity. Yet time and space are but inverse measures of the force of the soul. A man is capable of abolishing them both. The spirit sports with time—'Can crowd eternity into an hour, or stretch an hour to eternity.'...The emphasis of facts and persons to my soul has nothing to do with time. And so always the soul's scale is one; the scale of the senses and the understanding is another. Before the great revelations of the soul, Time, Space and Nature shrink away.... The soul looketh steadily forward, creating a world alway before her, leaving worlds alway behind her. She has no dates, nor rites, nor persons, nor specialties, nor men. The soul knows only the soul; all else is idle weeds for her wearing.... Within the same sentiment is the germ of intellectual growth, which obeys the same law.... For whoso dwells in this moral beatitude does already anticipate those special powers which men prize so highly...the heart which abandons itself to the Supreme Mind finds itself related to all its works, and will travel a royal road to particular knowledges and powers. For in ascending to this primary and aboriginal sentiment we have come from our remote station on the circumference instantaneously to the centre of the world, where...we see causes, and anticipate the universe, which is but a slow effect.

"This communication is an influx of the Divine Mind into our mind. It is an ebb of the individual rivulet before the flowing surges of the sea of life. Every distinct apprehension of this central commandment agitates men with awe and delight. A thrill passes through all men at the reception of new truth, or at the performance of a great action, which comes out of the heart of nature. In these communications the power to see is not separated from the will to do, but the insight proceeds from obedience, and the obedience proceeds from a joyful perception. Every moment when the individual feels himself invaded by it, it is memorable. Always, I believe, by the necessity of our constitution a certain enthusiasm attends the individual's consciousness of that divine presence. The character and duration of this enthusiasm varies with the state of the individual, from an ecstasy and trance and prophetic inspiration,—which is its rarer appearance, to the faintest glow of virtuous emotion, in which form it warms, like our household fires, all the families and associations of men, and makes society possible.... The trances of Socrates; the 'union' of Plotinus; the vision of Porphyry; the conversion of Paul; the aurora of Behmen; the convulsions of George Fox and his Quakers; the illumination of Swedenborg, are of this kind. What was in the case of these remarkable persons a ravishment, has, in innumerable instances in common life, been exhibited in less striking manner. Everywhere the history of religion betrays a tendency to enthusiasm. The raptures of the Moravian and Quietist; the opening of the internal sense of the Word, in the language of the New Jerusalem church; the revival of the Calvinistic churches; the experiences of the Methodists, are varying forms of that shudder of awe and delight with which the individual soul always mingles with the universal soul. The nature of these revelations is always the same; they are perceptions of the absolute law. They are solutions of the soul's own questions. They do not answer the questions which the understanding asks. The soul answers never by words, but by the thing itself that is inquired after.

"Thoughts come into our minds through avenues which we never left open, and thoughts go out of our minds through avenues which we never voluntarily opened... ...The great distinction between teachers sacred or literary; between poets like Herbert, and poets like Pope; between philosophers like Spinoza, Kant and Coleridge,—and philosophers like Locke, Paley, Macintosh and Stewart; between men of the world who are reckoned accomplished talkers, and here and there a fervent mystic, prophesying half-insane under the infinitude of his thought, is that one class speaks *from within*, or from experience, as parties and possessors of the fact; and the other class *from without*, as spectators merely, or perhaps as acquainted with the fact on the evidence of third persons. It is no use to preach to me from without. I can do that too easily myself. Jesus speaks always from within, and in a degree that transcends all others. In that is the miracle. That includes the miracle. My soul believes beforehand that it ought so to be.... The same Omniscience flows into the intellect and makes what we call genius. Much of the wisdom of the world is not wisdom, and the most illuminated class of men are no doubt superior to literary fame, and are not writers. Among the multitude of scholars and authors we feel no hallowing presence; we are sensible of a knack and skill rather than of inspiration; they have a light and know not whence it comes and call it their own; their talent is some exaggerated faculty, some overgrown member, so that their strength is a disease. In these instances the intellectual gifts do not make the impression of virtue, but almost of vice; and we feel that a man's talents stand in the way of his advancement in truth. But genius is religious. It is a larger imbibing of the common heart. It is not anomalous, more like and not less than other men. There is in all great poets a wisdom of humanity which is superior to any talents they exercise...This energy...comes to the lowly and simple; it comes to whomsoever will put off what is foreign and proud; it comes as insight; it comes as serenity and grandeur. When we see those whom it inhabits, we are apprised of new degrees of greatness. From that inspiration the man comes back with a changed tone. He does not talk with men with an eye to their opinion. He tries them. It requires of us to be plain and true.... Let man then learn the revelation of all nature and all thought to his heart; this namely that the Highest dwells with him; that the sources of nature are in his own mind, if the sentiment of duty is there.... The soul gives itself, alone, original and pure, to the Lonely, Original and Pure, who, on that occasion, gladly inhabits, leads and speaks through it. Then it is glad, young and nimble. It is not wise, but it sees through all things. It is not called religious, but it is innocent. It calls the light its own, and feels that the grass grows and the stone falls by a law inferior to, and dependent on, its nature. Behold, it saith, I am born into the great, the universal mind. I, the imperfect, adore my own Perfect. I am somehow receptive of the great soul, and thereby I do overlook the sun and the stars and feel them to be but the fair accidents and effects which change and pass. More and more the surges of everlasting nature enters into me, and I become public and human in my regards and actions. So come I to live in thoughts and act with energies which are immortal."

This essay of Emerson, from which we have quoted, contains perhaps the best illustration and example of the Western idea of the Transcendent Unity which manifests itself in the infinite variety of forms, shapes and centres of energy in the universe. And it is upon this general idea and conception that the various teachings regarding the Superconscious Mind are based. Resting upon this conception of the One Reality, is erected the edifice of thought which holds that the individual is but a centre of life, mind and activity in the great ocean of Life, and that in the course of evolution he is able to manifest more and still more of the qualities inherent in that Ocean—is enabled to unfold further that which is involved and latent within his soul.

Perhaps the most remarkable book on this subject, at least so far as the Western world is concerned, is that great work of Dr. Richard Maurice Bucke entitled "Cosmic Consciousness." Dr. Bucke held that just as life has evolved from sensation and the simpler forms of consciousness to what is known as "simple consciousness;" and then on to "self-consciousness" in its lower and higher forms; so is it pressing forward to a still wider and fuller plane of consciousness which he calls "Cosmic Consciousness," by which term he indicates the consciousness of a greater, grander and fuller life of which we form a part—the Universal Life of the Hindus, or the Over-Soul of Emerson. He claims that this consciousness will be developed and manifested fully by the race in the centuries to come, and that even now, here and there, are to be found individuals to whom have come moments of this consciousness—flashes from the Over-Soul. He holds that the wonderful religious and mystic experiences of people, in the past and in the present, in all lands and among all races, are but instances of this coming Cosmic Consciousness to which the race is moving.

Prof. William James in his work entitled "Some Varieties of Religious Experience" relates a number of instances of an unfolding consciousness of a Something Greater of which we are a Part—a Something, as Kipling expresses it: "So much more near than I had known, so much more great than I had guessed; and me like all the rest,—alone, but reaching out to all the rest." Bucke cites many examples in his work just mentioned and the pages of Mystic Philosophy are filled with instances of this kind. The temptation to enter further into this subject is great, but we must resist it for it is foreign to the field and scope of the present work. We, however, have given a hint to those who would pursue the subject still further.

In these theories regarding the Universal Mind, or Over Soul, may be found at least a reasonable explanation of the phenomena of the Superconscious—phenomena which have perplexed the orthodox psychologists. It is at least worthy of being given serious consideration, or of being used as a working hypothesis until some more reasonable theory is advanced. It is true that it carries one across the boundaries of ordinary psychology, into the realms of philosophy and metaphysics, if not indeed into the sacred regions of religion—but boundary lines are fast disappearing under the encroachments of modern scientific thought, and All indeed is becoming to be seen as but One in the end. As Prof. William James has said: "Pragmatism tends to *unstiffen* our theories. The world's oneness has generally been affirmed abstractly only, and as if anyone who questioned it must be an idiot. The temper of monists has been vehement, as almost at times to be convulsive; and this way of holding a doctrine does not easily go with reasonable discussion and the drawing of distinctions.... Pluralism on the other hand has no need of this dogmatic rigoristic temper. Provided that you grant *some* separation among things, some tremor of independence, some free play of parts on one another, some real novelty or chance, however minute, she is amply satisfied, and will allow you any amount, however great, of real union. How much of union there may be is a question that she thinks can be decided empirically.... This leaves us with the common-sense world, in which we find things partly joined, and partly disjoined." And so, you see, it is not necessary for one to become a Pantheist, or any similar "terrible thing" in order to accept, at least provisionally, the conception of a Oneness in which individuals are but evolving and unfolding parts of particles.

13
Unfolding the Superconscious.

Many writers and teachers have had much to say regarding the *development* of the Superconscious.

We feel that this term gives an entirely wrong impression of the nature of this wonderful region of the mind or soul, and consequently an erroneous idea regarding the process of awakening its activities. The Superconscious is not a faculty to be developed, for it is fully existent within us and merely awaits the day when its recognition will be complete. It is not a case of *developing* the Superconscious, but a case of developing *ourselves*.

The best authorities have compared this process of entering into a recognition, realization and manifestation of the higher regions of the mind as an *unfoldment*—an opening up akin to the unfolding of the rose from the bud. In the bud but the outward form is apparent, the real beauty of the full-blown rose being hidden away by the protecting sheaths or petals. And so it is with the human mind or soul. In the majority of persons but the outward expression is seen, the mental being being tightly folded up and the hidden beauties secreted from view so that their very existence is doubted. But in every human being there exists these higher phases of mind and soul. And the process of bringing them into manifestation is properly called an *unfoldment*.

The three stages of the unfoldment of the higher regions of the mind are as follows:

I. The Recognition.

II. The Realization.

III. The Manifestation.

The first stage, that of Recognition, is that being experienced by the majority of persons who experience the occasional flashes of "genius" or superconscious knowledge. In some cases, dimly—in other cases, plainly—this recognition is experienced.

The person begins to recognize the existence of new and unsuspected faculties or mental regions within himself. He may call this *intuition*, or inspiration, or genius, or by other terms in common use, but the cause underlying the phenomena is apparent to all who have studied along the lines of the New Psychology. It is the Superconscious in the process of unfoldment, striving to obtain recognition from the conscious mentality of the individuality, that it may take its proper place in the mental work of the evolving individual.

The most common form of this unfoldment is in the manifestation which we generally term *intuition*. Webster defines intuition as "Direct apprehension or cognition; immediate knowledge, as in perception or consciousness, involving no reasoning process; quick or ready insight or apprehension." Another writer has said: "Intuition is above the field of consciousness, and its messages are passed downward, though its processes are hidden. The race is gradually unfolding into the mental plane of Intuition, and will some day pass into full consciousness on that plane. In the meantime it gets but flashes and glimpses from the hidden region. Many of the best things we have, come from that region. Art, music, the love of the beautiful and good poetry, the higher form of love, spiritual insight to a certain degree, intuitive perception of truth, etc., come from this region. These things are not reasoned out by the intellect, but seem to spring full born from some unknown region of the mind."

One who wishes to aid in the unfoldment of the Superconscious, should strive to perfect this recognition. He should wait and watch for these messages from the higher regions of the self, and give them welcome when they come.

The greater the amount of recognition, the greater will be the response. This is but in accordance with nature as manifest in a thousand ways. Before one may avail himself of any mental or physical power he must first recognize the existence of that power within him, for otherwise it will as if he had it not. The Hindus speak of this mental state as akin to that of "the young elephant who does not know his own strength." Many persons have physical or mental strength or power, the existence of which they never suspect until some moment or occasion of great need brings the recognition which is quickly followed by the realization and manifestation. And so it is in the case of the Superconscious. One must first intellectually realize the existence of the regions of the mind before he may proceed further. The intellect is somewhat stubborn in this respect, and strives to fight against what it fancies to be an intruder upon its special domain. But this is a mistake, for the knowledge of the Superconscious does not run contrary to reason or the intellect—it merely transcends the latter. After a while the intellect begins to recognize it the Superconscious an elder brother—a helper and valuable aid. And, from that time harmony is established and the two work hand in hand for the common welfare of the individual.

Recognition of the Superconscious—the first step in its unfoldment—is accomplished simply by ceasing to interpose a resistance to the intuitive flashes on the part of the intellect.

This does not mean that the intellect should accept anything contrary to its own reasoning, but that it should welcome as a helper the intuitive faculties. The intellect should be willing to "take its own wherever it finds it," and to turn all to good account. If the Superconscious flashes a message to the intellect, the latter should proceed to investigate it, and if possible to turn it to account. Recognition must precede realization, and recognition is developed by *making welcome* the newcomer and inviting him to take a seat at the council table of the mind. When the intellect doubts and scorns the newcomer, the latter is apt to retreat and retrace its path, and dwell apart. What is needed is a thorough recognition of the truth expressed by a writer who said: "In the higher regions of the mind are locked up intuitive perceptions of all truth, and he who can gain access to these regions will know everything intuitively, and as a matter of clear sight, without reasoning or explanation." This attainment is Realization,—the belief in its possibility is Recognition.

Realization, the second step in unfoldment, is something higher than mere Recognition, although proceeding directly from the latter. It is very difficult to describe this Realization. Realization, you know, means: "The state of entering or bringing into actual existence, being or action; appreciating thoroughly and vividly in the mind," etc. In short means *the making real.* In this second step or stage the individual not only intellectually recognizes the existence of the Superconscious, but he also enters into a *knowing* on the plane of the Superconscious itself. He not only knows that the Superconscious *is*, by means of the intellect, but he also knows that it *is*, by reason of entering upon its own plane of knowing or consciousness. It is almost impossible to explain this to those who have not experienced it at least in a faint degree. It cannot be well described in the term of ordinary thought. It belongs to the unclassified and unnamed mental phenomena which the old psychology refused to admit. The old mystics and occultists understood it well, and have described it in glowing terms, as for instance, the following:

"Look for the flower to bloom in the silence that follows the storm; not till then. It shall grow, it will shoot up, it will make branches and leaves, and form buds while the storm lasts. But not until the entire personality of the man is dissolved and melted—not until it is held by the divine fragment which has created it, as a mere subject for grave experiment and experience—not until the whole nature has yielded and become subject to its higher self, can the bloom open. Then will come a calm such as comes in a tropical country after the heavy rain, when nature works so swiftly that one may see her action. Such a calm will come to the harassed spirit. And in the dead Silence will occur that which will prove that the war has been found. Call it by whatever name you will. It is a voice that speaks where there is none to speak, it is a messenger that comes—a messenger without form or substance—or it is the flower of the soul that has opened. It cannot be described by any metaphor. But it can be felt after, looked for and desired, even among the raging of the storm. The silence may last a moment of time, or it may last a thousand years. But it will end. Yet you will carry its strength with you. Again and again the battle must be fought and won. It is only for an interval that nature can be still."

If it is difficult to describe the stage of Recognition, what must we say regarding the final stage of Manifestation? Emerson, in his essay "The Oversoul," quoted from in the preceding chapter, has given us an idea of what life means to the individual who has entered into a conscious recognition and realization of the higher planes of the mind—the Greater Self—and we cannot expect to equal his beautiful description of that state. The very subject, in itself, is really beyond the scope and field of the present series of books on The New Psychology, but we have thought it advisable to touch lightly upon it in conclusion, that the interested student might realize the direction of the thought and spirit of the new movement or current of thought. We cannot speak of these higher regions as we would of the faculties of the conscious mind, for the reason that the subject has not reached that stage of scientific investigation in which new terms are applied and technical explanations are made by the highest authorities. At present the subject must rest in that dim light between scientific knowledge and fervent belief, and is more properly treated in poetic imagery and mystical terms— for there are no other terms available.

Accordingly, it is most proper to close the consideration by a quotation from Tennyson, who testified that he had entered in a full realization, and partial manifestation, of the Superconscious Knowing. He says of this:

"And more, my son, for more than once when I

Sat all alone, revolving in myself

That word which is the symbol of myself.

The mortal symbol of the self was loosed,

And passed into the Nameless, as a cloud

Melts into Heaven. I touched my limbs, the limbs

Were strange, not mine—and yet no shadow of doubt

But utter clearness, and through loss of Self

We gain of such large life as matched with ours

Were sun to spark, unshadowable in words,

Themselves but shadows of a shadow-world."

Finis.

Made in the USA
Middletown, DE
01 November 2023

41600814R00051